ENGLISH FOR ACCOUNTANCY

FRANCIS RADICE and JOHN ELLIOTT

PHOENIX
ELT
incorporating
PRENTICE HALL MACMILLAN

New York London Toronto Sydney Tokyo Singapore

First published in 1996 by Phoenix ELT
A division of Prentice Hall International (UK) Ltd
Campus 400, Spring Way
Maylands Avenue, Hemel Hempstead
Hertfordshire, HP2 7EZ

Typeset in the UK
by Charles Design Associates
Printed by Progressive Printing (UK) Ltd., Leigh-on-Sea, Essex
Illustrated by Peter Kent

British Library Cataloguing in Publication Data

A catalogue record for this book is available from the British Library.

ISBN 0-13-407461 0

5 4 3 2 1
1999 98 97 96

Contents

UNIT		PAGE
1	Turnover Trouble	5
2	A Question of Figures	16
3	How Much Does It Cost?	30
4	Doubtful Ratios	44
5	The Way Forward	56
6	Evaluating a Project	75
7	Reviewing the Financial Base	88
8	Obtaining Finance	103
9	The Path to Partnership	118
10	Deciding on Partners	133
	Tapescripts	146
	Answer Key	153
	Glossary	172
	Index	185

ACKNOWLEDGEMENT

The authors and publishers wish to thank the Department of Business Administration, University of Delaware, for permission to reproduce the Index for the Analysis of Country Risks in Unit 6 of this book.

UNIT 1 Turnover Trouble

A Introduction

This unit practises the English you need to understand and discuss:

1 A problem of falling profits during increased turnover
2 Some of the figures in a Profit and Loss statement
3 How to determine the break-even point.

This course is based on a case study of a company in Manara, an imaginary island state in the West. Its capital is Manara City and its currency is the Manara dollar (M$).

The story begins with the financial problems of Proteus (Manara) Ltd, the Manara-based subsidiary of a multinational company. It moves through proposing solutions to these problems to the eventual setting up of a joint venture company in Eastern Europe.

... A 20 per cent increase in turnover

B Discussion I

Before reading

1. What do you know about the following terms?
   turnover gross margin net profit gross profit
2. How might it be possible for a company to have an increasing turnover and decreasing profits at the same time?

C Reading I

Turnover trouble

The Proteus Group plc is an electrical engineering company based in Birmingham. It makes electrical equipment for street lighting, public buildings and sports stadiums. It is a public limited company whose shares are listed on the London Stock Exchange.

Proteus has subsidiaries in several countries. One of these companies, Proteus (Manara) Limited, makes the Protocap – an energy saver which helps to economise on electricity used for public lighting.

One day in January the Managing Director was studying the management accounts. He noticed with alarm that his net profits had fallen, although the accounts showed a 20 per cent increase in turnover over the last year.

He was pleased with the increased sales to Central and Eastern Europe. These had risen despite the recession. He had achieved this increase by lowering the price of his main product, the Protocap Energy Saver. As a result, the gross margin had fallen from 31 per cent to 14 per cent of sales. His financial plan had been to increase sales of other products and and thus maintain his overall gross profit. He had, however, paid a price increase to one of his suppliers. This reduced his gross margin on other products by 2 per cent to 29 per cent. Now his net profit had fallen, and this worried him.

D Vocabulary

1 Choose the best explanation to show the meaning of each of the expressions below. Words are marked for stress, to help you with pronunciation.

a) **sub<u>sid</u>iary** (*n*)
i) company owned by another company
ii) branch of a company
iii) agent of a company in another country
iv) money paid by the government to help a company or industry

b) **turnover** (*n*)
i) total value of production in one year
ii) complete change of production methods
iii) total value of sales in one period of time
iv) change from making a big loss to making a profit

c) **gross profit** (*adj + n*)
The income of a business after the deduction of:
i) all the production costs (e.g. raw materials, fuel, finished and unfinished goods in store, overheads, factory and direct labour costs)
ii) income tax
iii) overheads
iv) all operating expenses and tax

d) **net profit** (*adj + n*)
The income of a business after deduction of:
i) all operating expenses
ii) tax
iii) overheads
iv) all operating expenses, costs of sales and tax

e) **gross margin** (*adj + n*)
i) the difference between selling price and cost of manufacture, minus factory overheads
ii) a large-scale production method used in some countries
iii) the same as gross profit
iv) the total value of goods remaining unsold at the end of the year

f) **overall gross profit** (*adjs + n*)
i) money remaining after all costs including tax have been deducted
ii) same as net profit
iii) same as gross profit
iv) excess profit over previously estimated figure

2 How are the following ideas expressed in the passage?

a) Several companies together with one holding company (*1 word, paragraph 1*)
b) With its head office in (Birmingham) (*2 words, paragraph 1*)
c) A company whose investors cannot lose more than the money they have invested in it, and in which anyone may invest (*3 words, paragraph 1*)
d) The chief UK share market (*3 words, paragraph 1*)
e) The chief of a company who is also a shareholder in it (*2 words, paragraph 3*)
f) Financial information used by the people running a company (*2 words, paragraph 3*)
g) Period of economic downturn (*1 word, paragraph 4*)
h) The opposite of customers (*1 word, paragraph 4*)
i) Absorbed (*1 word, paragraph 4*)

E Listening I

Look at the incomplete dialogue below. Listen to the conversation on the cassette, which practises the vocabulary introduced in Reading I. Then complete the script.

Dialogue 1

The Managing Director (MD) of Proteus Manara is explaining the situation to the new accountant (A):

A So you're a .... of the Proteus .... which is .... Birmingham?
MD That's right. We're a .... and our .... are quoted on the London ....
A You must be doing well. I see the .... show a 20 per cent .... in .... !
MD That's true but we also had a .... in our ....
A Oh, I see. Can you explain how that happened?
MD I'm not sure. You see, despite the .... our .... to Eastern Europe ....
A So income from sales should have risen.
MD Yes, but we only .... sales by .... the price of our main product. So our .... from 31 per cent to 14 per cent of sales.
A So your income from .... but your profits .... !
MD I know. We hope to make them rise by .... sales of other .... and .... our .... But we had to .... a price .... by one of our .... and this .... our .... on our other products by 2 per cent. Now our .... has ....

F Grammar

Omitting the relative pronoun

....based in Birmingham

1 Look at these examples:

A Proteus is an engineering company. The base of the company is in Birmingham.

To avoid repetition and to provide a description which identifies the company, the writer has made one sentence:

B Proteus is an engineering *company based in* Birmingham.

2 Now rewrite the following pairs of sentences in the same way.

a) The Protocap has components. Sub-contractors supply the components.
b) They make electric cars. They equip the electric cars with battery chargers
c) The accountant showed us the half yearly results. They had prepared the results for the board meeting.
d) They were drinking wine. Someone had imported the wine from Hungary.

e) He was worried by the fall in net profit. Reduced margins of their main products caused this fall.
f) In the financial plan he decided to increase the sales of their secondary products. He submitted the plan to the head office in Birmingham.
g) The Protocap was cheaper to produce in Manara than in Birmingham. Proteus' subsidiary company made the Protocap.

whose shares are listed on the London Stock Exchange (*line* 4)

The sentence is made up of two parts:

A It is a public limited company.
\+ Its shares are listed on the Stock Exchange.
= It is a public limited company *whose* shares are listed on the Stock Exchange.

B Mr Walker gave the first lecture.
\+ His books are read by all those working in public finance.
= Mr Walker, *whose* books are read by all those working in public finance, gave the first lecture.

3 Now join the following pairs of sentences in the same way.

a) There are hundreds of accountants.
Their addresses can be found in the 'phone book.
b) It's a large engineering company.
Its factories make components for car manufacturers.
c) They are exporters of foodstuff.
Their supermarkets are all over the country.
d) He bought shares in BM Engineering.
Their value fell soon after he bought them.
e) There were hundreds of passengers in the departure lounge.
Their flights had been delayed by the fog.
f) They were worried about the company.
Its production costs had risen sharply.
g) Production was delayed at the factory.
Its main building had been damaged by a recent fire.
h) The government lowered interest rates.
Its economic policy had failed.
i) The manager wanted to know why the company was making less profit.
The company's turnover had increased.
j) The Financial Controller said that prices must be raised.
The Financial Controller's advice had been asked.

Despite

Note the use of 'despite' in paragraph 4.

4 Choose the best word to complete each of the following sentences.

a) The accountant said that profits would increase despite the fall in .... *gross margins / overheads / turnover.*
b) Turnover should be cut despite .... *healthy sales / current liabilities / creditors.*

c) Prices were lowered despite an increase in .... *suppliers / costs / stocks.*
d) He hoped to maintain overall profit despite .... *smaller margins / increased sales / creditors.*
e) He did absorb a price increase despite .... *gross margins / his lowering his price / his overall profit.*

Transitive and intransitive verbs

The following verbs are transitive and *must* take an object:

lower (*line 14*), reduce (*line 18*), make (*lines 2 and 6*), list (*line 4*), raise, have, use.

Examples:
They lowered my wages.
He reduced the number of cigarettes he smoked.
She listed my mistakes.

The following verbs are intransitive and *cannot* take an object:

fall (*line 15*), rise (*line 13*), go up / down.

Examples:
The sun rises every morning.
Share prices fell.

Some verbs may be used transitively or intransitively and may take an object or not; one of these is 'increase' (*line 16*).

Examples:
The government increased public spending.
Each year the money supply increases.

When you look up verbs in English dictionaries, you often find them marked *vi* (intransitive verb) or *vt* (transitive verb).

5 Choose a grammatically correct verb for each sentence. (In each case, more than one verb is acceptable.)

a) Profits had / *fallen / lowered / decreased / reduced.*
b) The government's policy had / *fallen / lowered / decreased / reduced /* profits.
c) Profits had / *risen / raised / increased / gone up.*
d) He hoped that a change of policy would / *rise / raise / increase /* profits.

6 Insert the correct verb forms in the following sentences.

a) A price increase by one of his suppliers .... his margin from 31 per cent to 29 per cent.
b) Sales had .... despite the recession.
c) The company's accounts .... a 20 per cent .... in turnover.
d) The company's accounts .... a .... in profits from 20 per cent to 5 per cent.

e) Sales could .... by 37 per cent and the company would still make a profit.
f) Now profits .... and this worried him.
g) What you've got to do is .... your turnover!
h) .... output of the Protocap and increase your margin.
i) He had achieved this by .... the price on his main product.
j) It'll be pretty bad especially if our overheads .... (*2 words*) and our overall sales margin ....

G Discussion II

Comprehension

Ask and answer questions with your colleagues.

What does Proteus do?
Where is it based?
What does it make?
What happened recently?

What is a public limited company?
a Managing Director?
the London Stock Exchange?
the net profit?
the gross margin?
turnover?
What are management accounts?

H Reading II

An extract from a memorandum

Extract from a memorandum from the newly-appointed Financial Controller of Proteus (Manara) to his Managing Director on the latest monthly financial report:-

> ..... the strong export sales in the last six months improved our overall sales total for the year. But we have not generated enough gross profit to cover all our operating and financial expenses.
>
> Our return on capital is now well below the minimum set by Head Office. This arises from low profit and excess working capital as the attached Balance Sheet shows.
>
> Better reporting on product profitability is essential, particularly in the area of production costing, in order to identify those products with a low gross profit .....

I Vocabulary

1 Identify the more formal phrases in the passage which have the following meanings.

a)	Part of a memo	*(4 words)*
b)	Our big export sales figures	*(4 words)*
c)	We haven't made enough money	*(7 words)*
d)	All costs of the business	*(4 words)*
e)	Income from money invested	*(3 words)*
f)	This comes from having ...	*(3 words)*
g)	Too much money being used in the business	*(3 words)*
h)	Giving more details about ...	*(2 words)*
i)	The profit-making power of a product	*(2 words)*
j)	We have to pick out ...	*(4 words)*

2 Choose the best verb to complete each of the sentences below.

a) The company's profitability has / *got better* / *increased* / *benefited* / *improved*.
b) The company's profits have / *got better* / *increased* / *benefited* / *improved*.
c) I'm not making enough money to / *pay for* / *cover* / *absorb* / *finance* / all my business expenses.
d) I'm not making enough money to / *pay for* / *cover* / *absorb* / *finance* / extra costs.
e) We need to / *identify* / *pinpoint* / *name* / *find* / the products which are losing money.
f) We need to / *identify* / *pinpoint* / *name* / *find* / the cause of the problem.
g) The business needs to / *create* / *build up* / *produce* / *generate* / enough profit to pay for operating and financial costs.
h) The sales manager / *set* / *stated* / *gave* / *submitted* / the target for the next six months.

3 Without looking back at Reading II, find one word to fill each space.

Extract from a memorandum from the newly appointed Financial (1).......... of Proteus (Manara) to his Managing (2).......... on the latest monthly financial report:

The (3).......... export sales in the last six (4)......... improved our overall sales total for (5).......... year. But we have not generated enough gross profit to cover all our (6)......... and financial expenses.

Our return on (7).......... is now well below the minimum (8).......... by Head Office. This arises from (9).......... profit and excess working capital as (10).......... attached Balance Sheet shows.

Better reporting (11).......... product profitability is essential, particularly in the area of (12).......... costing, in order to identify those (13).......... with a low gross profit .....

J Use of vocabulary

Look at the incomplete dialogue below, which covers the content of the memorandum in Reading II. Then listen to the conversation on tape and complete the script.

Dialogue 2

The Financial Controller (FC) of Proteus (Manara) Ltd telephones the Managing Director (MD):

FC I just wanted to say something about that .... I gave you.

MD Yes, I think I see what's wrong. The .... were good but not good enough.

FC That's right. Our .... did not make enough to .... all our costs.

MD Yes, I can see that the .... is now well below the .... set by Head Office. How did that happen?

FC Well, it's because of the low profit, you see. And .... It's clear from the Balance Sheet.

MD Hm, I see. So what do you think we should do about it?

FC Well, we must .... on how much profit each product makes. This applies particularly to .... ; so we can see which products .... a low .... and which products are doing well ....

K Listening for information

Dialogue 3

After reading the Financial Controller's memorandum, the Managing Director called him in for a more detailed discussion of the problem.

Read the questions below and listen to the discussion on tape. Then listen to the discussion again and write the answers to the questions.

Note: Cost of Sales = manufacturing costs.
Operating expenses = administration and marketing costs.
See Glossary for more detail.

1 What wasn't clear to the Managing Director?
2 The Managing Director mentions two extra production costs. What are they?
3 How much had the sales increased from the previous year?
4 What financial document does the Financial Controller mention?

5 The Financial Controller mentions an increased cost.
What type of costs had increased?
6 What accountancy concept does the Financial Controller mention, which will help them to understand the question?
7 Can you say what the break-even point is?
8 What was the figure for sales, the year before last?
9 What was the figure for gross profit?
10 What was the figure for operating expenses for the same year?
11 What was the break-even point for the same year?
12 What does the break-even point tell you about what the company needs to do?

L Problem-solving

The following tasks test your understanding of the conversation between the Proteus Managing Director and his Financial Controller.

1 Here are the relevant figures for the last year's Profit and Loss Account. Calculate the break-even point:

	1993 (M$000)	*1994* (M$000)
Sales	2,000	2,400
Cost of sales	1,380	1,750
Gross profit	620	650
% of sales	31%	27%
Operating expenses	520	630

2 Complete the diagram below. Mark the break-even point.

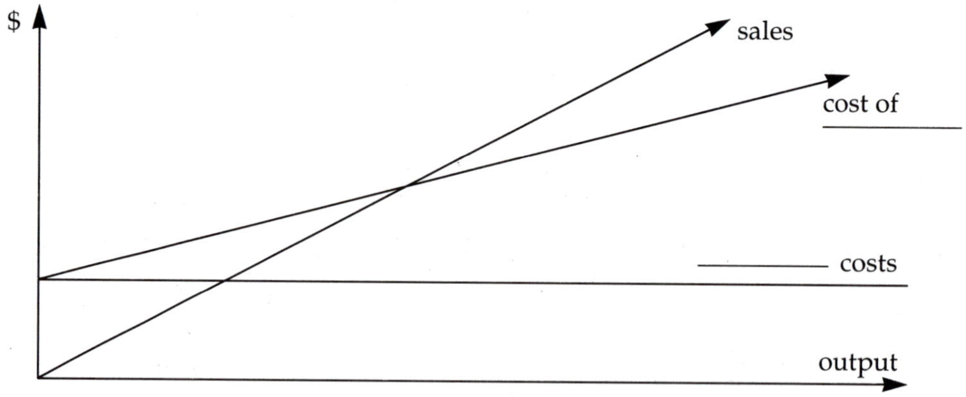

3 Why does Proteus Manara need to sell much more in 1995?

M Listening and note-taking

Listen to the dialogue again. Imagine that you are assisting the Managing Director and are about to attend a meeting of the shareholders. Use the outline notes below to prepare a short report for the shareholders.

PROTEUS MANARA LTD

MEMO

Good news:	Increased .... to Central and Eastern Europe
Problems:	Fall in ....
	Increased warehousing and.......... costs
Possible causes:	.... have increased faster than income
	Smaller ....
Solutions:	Reduce ....
	Increase ....

UNIT 2 A Question of Figures

A Introduction

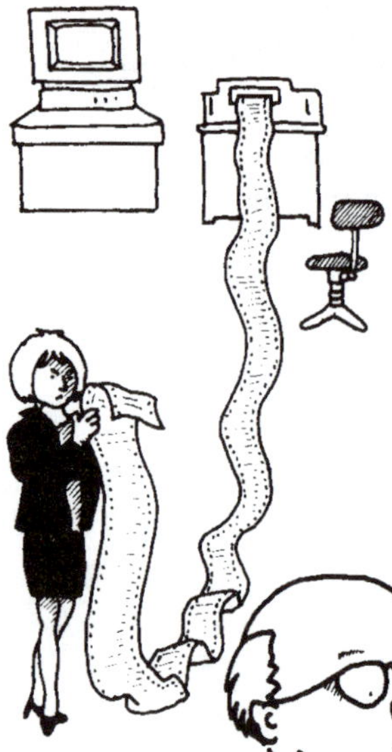

The story so far

The Managing Director of Proteus, an electrical engineering company in Manara, a country in the West, has discovered that his accounts show a fall in profits despite a rise in turnover. His accountant, the Financial Controller of the company, has told him that the solution to the problem would become clear after they have analysed the Profit and Loss statements and the Balance Sheet.

This unit practises the English you need to understand and discuss:

a A Profit and Loss Account
b A Balance Sheet

...The solution would become clear after they had analysed the profit and loss statements and the balance sheet

B Discussion I

Before reading

Working in small groups, take it in turns to say what you know about the terms below, using the words in brackets and other words which have appeared in Unit 1. Can you explain what they mean?

1. Profit and Loss Account (income, expenditure, period, year)
2. Balance Sheet (photograph, condition, point in time)
3. Opening inventory (raw materials, unfinished goods, unsold stock, beginning of the accounting period)
4. Factory overheads (administration, heating, electricity, costs)

C Reading I

Profit and loss account

INTERNAL MANAGEMENT REPORTING

PROFIT AND LOSS STATEMENT

('000 Manara dollars)

	1993	*1994*
SALES	2,000	2,400
COST OF SALES		
Opening inventory	230	250
Purchases	1,100	1,480
	1,330	1,730
Closing inventory	250	350
	1,080	1,380
Labour costs	190	245
Factory overheads	110	125
Total cost of sales	1,380	1,750
GROSS PROFIT	620	650
% of sales	31%	27%
OPERATING EXPENSES		
Selling/distribution	350	440
Administration	150	160
Interest costs	20	30
	520	630
PROFIT BEFORE TAX	100	20
TAXATION @ 40%	40	8
NET PROFIT	60	12

D Vocabulary

Choose the best explanation to show the meaning of each of the expressions below. Words are marked for stress, to help you with pronunciation.

1 **cost of sales**
Note: This term is used for all the items listed in this Profit and Loss statement rather than production costs mentioned in Unit 1 D 1 (page 7).

2 **opening inventory** (*adj + n*)
a) The value of raw materials, components, spare parts, work in progress and fuel at the beginning of an accounting period
b) All the supplies, goods and raw materials that are used to set up a business
c) unsold goods left over from previous financial years
d) The value of raw materials, components, spare parts, finished products, work in progress and fuel at the beginning of an accounting period

3 **factory overheads** (*n*)
a) Costs of fuel, raw materials and components
b) Other costs not directly concerned with production
c) Costs of water, electricity and fuel used in factory buildings
d) Depreciation on all machinery, equipment and stock
e) a) + c)
f) Costs of transport from the factory
g) b) + c) + d)

4 **interest costs**
Costs of
a) marketing b) sales c) advertising d) borrowing

E Grammar

The Proteus Profit and Loss Account: Practice with numbers

1 Ask and answer questions about the information in the profit and loss account, as in the example. Note that when saying numbers, we say 'a hundred *and* ten' and so on.

Examples

What was the figure for opening inventory in 1993?
Two hundred and thirty thousand Manara dollars.

What is the figure for closing inventory in 1994?
Three hundred and fifty thousand Manara dollars.

What was the total cost of sales in 1993?
One million, three hundred and eighty thousand Manara dollars.

What about gross profit in 1994?
It comes to six hundred and fifty thousand Manara dollars.

Language for calculation: percentages and return on capital

2 Calculate the net profit for 1993 as a percentage of sales.

Example 1993

$\frac{60}{2,000} \times 100 = 3\%$

Sixty over two thousand times a hundred
or Sixty divided by two thousand times a hundred
equals three per cent

Now explain the calculation for 1994 in words.

Using *by* .... *to* ....

3 Note the penultimate sentence of the reading passage on page 6:

This reduced his gross margin by 2 per cent to 29 per cent.

Make four similar sentences based on the information in the profit and loss Account, as in the example:

Example

Sales rose by / went up by / increased by M$400,000 to 2,400,00 in 1994.

		1993	*1994*
SALES		2,000	2,400
COST OF SALES			
	Opening inventory	230	250
	Purchases	1,100	1,480
		1,330	1,730
	Closing inventory	250	350
		1,080	1,380
	Labour costs	190	245
	Factory overheads	110	125
	Total cost of sales	1,380	1,750
GROSS PROFIT		620	650
	% of sales	31%	27%
OPERATING EXPENSES			
	Selling/distribution	350	440
	Administration	150	160
	Interest costs	20	30
		520	630
PROFIT BEFORE TAX		100	20

Using *There is/are, was/were, has been/have been, will be*

4 Change the following sentences to begin with *There / is / are / was / will be / has been*. Use the notes to help you.
Note: We do not normally use 'There exists ....', although it is not actually incorrect.

a) Overheads increased. (..... an increase in .....)
b) Proteus has several subsidiaries in other countries.
c) Net profits actually fell. (..... a fall in .....)
d) Sales to Central and Eastern Europe rose. (.....a rise in .....)
e) The gross margin on the Protocap was 31 per cent. (..... gross margin of .....)
f) Now the margin is only 14 per cent (..... a margin of only .....)
g) One of the suppliers increased prices. (..... an increase in .....)
h) Another problem exists.
i) You will make a saving in production costs.
j) Sales will fall by 37 per cent.

F Listening I

Read the incomplete dialogue below. Listen to the conversation on the cassette, which practises the vocabulary introduced in Reading I. Then complete the script.

The Managing Director continues his discussion with the Financial Controller:

FC Now in last year's figures, there was a 20 per cent .... The worst increase was in .... paid to the bank because of government stupidity in .... interest rates.

MD Then, of course, ... went up, but .... seven and a half ....

FC Yes, these .... wouldn't have been so bad but for the large .... These, together with the .... in .... and factory ...., ... the total cost of sales by ....

MD This meant our .... to only 27 per cent of sales. And the .... rose to $2,333,000, an increase of 39 per cent .... last year's figure.

FC In other words you would have needed an .... $633,000 of sales just to .... in your ....

G Reading II

PROTEUS MANARA LTD
Balance Sheet (000 Manara dollars)

	1993	*1994*
FIXED ASSETS		
Land and buildings	30	29
Plant and equipment	350	460
Vehicles	110	130
	490	619
CURRENT ASSETS		
Inventories	250	350
Receivables	420	550
Bank balance	70	<134>
	740	766
CURRENT LIABILITIES		
Payables	320	429
Tax payable on profits	40	8
Taxes payable	20	32
Short-term loans	70	124
	450	593
CAPITAL EMPLOYED	780	792
FINANCED BY		
Share capital	500	500
Retained profits	280	292
SHAREHOLDERS' EQUITY	780	792

H Vocabulary and dictionary work

1 Choose the best explanation to show the meaning of each expression. Words are marked for stress, to help you with pronunciation.

Fixed assets

a) Money, financial investments and services owed to a company
b) Goods, goodwill, capital, land, buildings, vehicles and machinery which a company owes to others
c) Goods, goodwill, capital, land, buildings, vehicles and machinery which a company owns
d) a) + b)
e) a) + c)

Debtors and creditors Which is which?

f) People who owe the company money
g) People to whom the company owes money

Shareholders' equity

h) Money distributed to the workers as a bonus
i) The money invested in the business by the owners
j) Capital contributed by investors in the Stock Exchange
k) Surplus wealth generated by the business

Discussion

2 a) Which items in the box below should be classed as fixed assets and which ones as current assets?

money in the bank	raw materials	factory buildings	
lorries	machinery	unpaid invoices	unsold stock

b) Match the terms on the left with the definitions on the right.

Payables	Unsettled customer accounts, trade credits received
Receivables	Unsold goods, spare parts for machines, unfinished parts
Inventories	Electricity bill, telephone bill

Definitions

3 Read out one of the definitions below and choose someone to find the matching word.
(*Note* The definitions given here are approximate only. For more detail, or to settle disputes, see your accountancy lecturer.)

a) raw materials, finished goods, work in progress, components
b) total invoiced sales of goods or services, less the value of returned goods minus trade discounts and credits
c) a short-term borrowing facility provided by a bank, enabling a business or person to draw money up to a certain limit
d) any resource owned by the company which can be valued in money terms
e) amounts owed to the business
f) a statement of the assets, liabilities and shareholders' funds at a certain time on a certain date
g) opposite of a loss
h) cost which is not directly related to production of the goods or services being sold by a firm
i) amounts owed by the business
j) all debts of a business, including dividends owed to the shareholders
k) money, property and assets used in a business
l) company which is owned by a parent company
m) difference between the cost of a product and the selling price
n) record of business transactions in money paid or owed

I Phrase building

Adjective-noun phrases

1 Start by choosing from the list of nouns and then add appropriate adjectives to make 3-word phrases. (The numbers in brackets show how many of the adjectives can be used with each noun.)

	Adjectives	Nouns	
	annual	profit	(5)
	large	margin	(3)
	gross	overheads	(1)
	net	stock	(5)
	fixed	assets	(6)
a	current	debtors	(1)
the	production	creditors	(3)
my	sales	liabilities	(5)
another	substantial	overdraft	(2)
our	valuable	capital	(2)
your	opening	turnover	(5)
....			
	healthy		
	company	subsidiary	(3)
	bank	increase	(3)
	sales	account	(5)
	overseas	Balance Sheet	(2)
	profit		

Verb-adjective-noun phrases

2 Now make 4-word phrases by choosing verbs from the box and adding them to the adjective-noun phrases you made above:

Examples
Last year they *made a substantial profit.*
So they *had a healthy balance sheet.*

increase	have	calculate	make	reduce
lower	purchase	raise	accumulate	

J Grammar

Talking about calculations

multiply by, deduct from, subtract from, add to

1 Use the information in the Profit and Loss Account and Balance Sheet to make sentences like the example.

Example
.... break-even point .....(divide).........
overheads to/by/from ..... gross margin as a percentage of sales.

You could work out your break-even point by *dividing your* overheads *by your* gross margin as a percentage of sales.

a) .... gross profit .....(multiply)..... units sold to/by/from .... margin.
b) .... overheads .....(deduct)..... production costs to/by/from .... total costs.
c) .... net profit .....(subtract)..... tax to/by/from .... gross profit.
d) .... current assets .....(add)..... stock to/by/from .... debtors.

Now make your own examples without the help of notes.

e) You can .... your current liabilities by ....
f) .... work out .... net assets by ....
g) .... total liabilities by ....

K Listening for information

Return on capital

An accountant explains how to calculate return on capital.

Read the questions below and listen to the tape. Then listen to the tape again and write answers to the questions.

1. What is one of the purposes of the Balance Sheet?
2. Explain what return on capital is.
3. Why are shareholders interested in the return on capital?
4. What does the capital of a company consist of?
5. If the capital shown on the Balance Sheet of 31.12.93 was M$780,000 and the capital shown on the Balance Sheet of 31.12.94 was M$792,000 and the net profit after tax was M$12,000, what was the return on capital for 1993 – 1994?

L Listening II

What should the Managing Director do?

In Unit 1 we found that the 1994 Balance Sheet figures showed a break-even point which was too high to cover the increased operating expenses without substantially increased sales.

In a subsequent meeting, the Managing Director of Proteus (Manara) Ltd (MD) and the Financial Controller (FC) continue their discussion. The Managing Director wants to know what to do.

First read the incomplete tapescript. Listen to the tape. Then listen to it again and complete the script.

MD OK. I understand what you're saying, but what do you think caused the fall in the ....? I thought that .... of the Protocap Energy Saver would produce .... But the opposite has happened.

FC Yes, clearly the gross margin on the Protocap is too low. We must look at the figures .... – especially the costs.

MD That reminds me. Our .... costs – the bank manager rang me yesterday saying that he was worried about the .... Why has our borrowing gone up so much since last year?

FC Well, mainly because we've been borrowing .... and the costs of extra .... and .... Let's have a quick look at the 1993 Balance Sheet.

MD All right. But make it quick! I've got a meeting with a customer in ten minutes.

FC Well, this shouldn't take a minute. Our .... were 40 per cent higher in 1994 than in 1993 and the .... were up by 31 per cent. But note that .... only 20 per cent. So we must .... more effectively.
On the other hand we ended 1994 .... 38 per cent more than in 1993, so the .... you got from them was financing .... in the current assets. The rest, $90,000, was .... the extra money we borrowed from our bank.

MD Yes, I see. But can you give me any suggestions for action now? I want to tell the managers as soon as possible.

FC Well, I suppose we could .... the Protocap Energy Saver, and try to .... all the other products. That would reduce our turnover, but it would certainly ....

MD .... turnover! Is this some kind of joke? What do you think Head Office in Birmingham would say?

FC No, I'm quite serious. Just think about it. Our sales .... but we'll be selling mostly products .... I know we won't be able to reduce some costs, particularly .... – they don't change with the sales volume, but overall we would end up with more dollars of profit. And our return on capital ....

MD That's rather difficult to follow. Could you go over that again?

FC Certainly! It's easy to work out. If we could raise our gross margin to 33 per cent ....

M Vocabulary

1 Match each of the phrases from Listening II with the correct explanation.

Phrases

a) borrowing costs	i) paid for
b) overdraft	ii) unpaid suppliers
c) working capital	iii) labour
d) storage	iv) money used to pay business expenses
e) personnel	v) the number of items sold
f) trade creditors	vi) warehousing
g) covered	vii) interest
h) sales volume	viii) money owed to the bank on current account

Collocations

2 Match the words on the left with those on the right to make 2-word nouns.

borrowing	capital
extra	receivables
extra	storage
customer	costs
working	personnel

N Grammar

Showing understanding and agreement

Look at the underlined examples from the conversation.

We must increase our gross margins. (*understand, say*)
I understand what you're saying.

Our operating costs have risen too rapidly. (*can see, happen*)
I can see what is happening.

1 Make similar statements in the same way.

a) We must keep records of production costs of each item. (*see, mean*)
b) Reduce turnover! You can't be serious! (*know, feel*)
c) We'll have to increase the sales of the more profitable items and reduce sales of the less profitable items. (*see, drive at*)
d) It's a question of reducing operating costs. (*appreciate, say*)

Indirect thought or speech about doubtful events

Would is used to express tentative or hypothetical prediction in the past.

Example
I (think) that extra sales of the Protocap Energy Saver (produce) even more profit.
I *thought* that extra sales of the Protocap Energy Saver *would produce* even more profit. (*lines* 2-3)

2 Use the notes to write your own examples.

a) If we (cut) turnover, what do you think Head Office in Birmingham (say)?
b) He (hope) the increased export sales (pay) for the increased overheads.
c) The Financial Controller (explain) it (be) necessary to cut turnover.
d) The Managing Director said he (understand) better if the Financial Controller (explain) everything again.
e) The Managing Director (hope) the accountant (provide) the answers.

Indirect thought or speech about prior events

Here, the event happened *before* the time of speaking.

Example
The Financial Controller (note) sales ..... (rise) by only 20 per cent.
The Financial Controller *noted* that sales *had risen* by only 20 per cent.

3 Use the notes to write your own examples.

a) The Managing Director (think) there (be) a mistake.
b) The accountant (explain) gross margins (become) too small.
c) He (realise) something (go) wrong.
d) The accountant (think) not everything (be understood).
e) The Production Manager (say) not all the parts (arrive).

Indirect thought or speech about simultaneous events in the past

Note that the tenses of the verbs in the example show that two events (phoning and being worried) happened at the same time:

Example
The bank manager *phoned* saying that he *was* worried about the increase in our overdraft. (*lines 7-8*)

4 Rewrite these sentences, using the correct tense of the verbs in brackets.

a) The accountant (tell) the manager the situation (be) urgent.
b) The customer (say) he (want) the Protocaps immediately.
c) He (realise) it (be) possible to reduce turnover and increase profits.
d) They (understand) the problem (lie) in a reduction of costs.
e) The accountant (become) aware the Managing Director (have to) go and meet the customer.

Indirect thought or speech about definite future events

When there is certainty about the future event, the simple future with *will* is used.

Example
I *know* we *won't* be able to reduce some costs. (*lines 32-33*)

5 Use the notes to write your own examples.

a) He (think) it (be) impossible to increase sales.
b) She (say) she (come) to the meeting.
c) I (hope) I (see) you when you come to England.

Past actions leading to the present situation

The present perfect tense is used for past events with present results.

Example
Proteus' borrowing has gone up substantially since last year.
I thought profits would rise. But the opposite has happened.

6 Use the notes to write your own examples.

a) There (be) an increase in operating costs.
b) We (take on) more production line workers.
c) Exports to Western Europe (rise).
d) The Chief Accountant (make) a report on the situation.
e) It (become) necessary to reduce sales of the items which cost more to produce.

But note the following exception:

Have got / 've got has the same form as the present perfect but it is used for the present.

I've got a meeting with a customer in ten minutes. (*lines 13-14*)

This is a special form of the present simple equivalent to the American English:

I have a meeting with a customer in ten minutes.

Continuous past actions leading to the present situation

The present perfect continuous is used for actions which have been going on for some time and have a present importance.

Example
Well, mainly because we've been borrowing extra working capital. (*line 10*)

7 Use the notes to write your own examples.

a) He (drink) beer all night long.
b) He (talk) on the telephone since lunchtime.
c) The break-even point (rise) during the past year.
d) Trade between East and West (grow) recently.
e) Work on the dam (continue).

Qualifying the verb

Note the adverbial phrase in the example:

Example
We must look at the figures *in more detail*, especially the costs. (*lines 5-6*)

8 Make your own examples by joining the adverbial phrases on the right to the main sentences on the left. Rewrite the sentences in full.

The costs should be examined	more clearly
It doesn't pay to do things	more accurately
The calculation could be done	in such a hurry
So we must control our working capital	with greater care
The accountant explained everything again	more effectively

O Explanations Game

Participants ask other members of the group to give explanations of terms which have occurred in this unit. For example:

Term	*Explanation*
Inventory	List of unfinished goods, parts, fuel or other items used for production

UNIT 3 How Much Does It Cost?

A Introduction

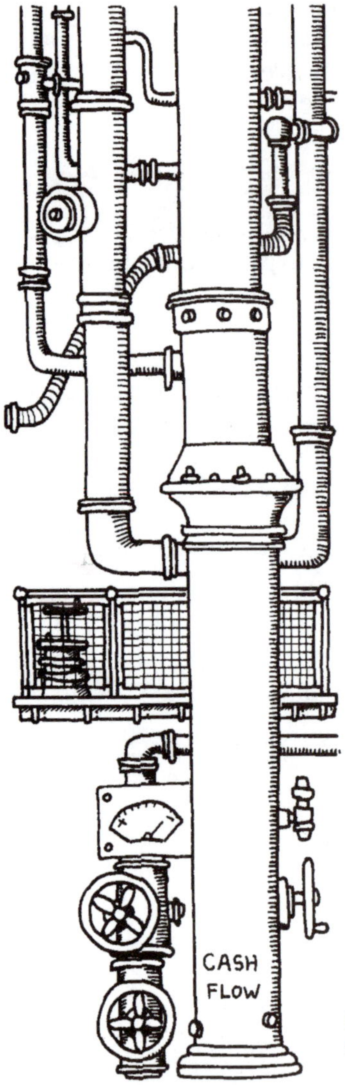

The story so far

The Managing Director (MD) of Proteus, the Manaran subsidiary of a Birmingham electrical engineering company, learned in January 1995 that, in spite of increasing sales, his net profit had fallen.

His Financial Controller (FC) explained that the fall in profits was caused by the MD's recent decision to reduce the price of his main product - the Protocap Energy Saver. Although this gained a bigger market share, it reduced profits and raised the break-even point, because of increases in fixed costs and reduced margins.

The other serious problem for the MD was Proteus's cash flow. The result of reduced profit margins and additional expenses had been less cash inflow. Also he was under pressure from his bank to reduce his overdraft. His FC told him to improve his gross margins by cutting sales of the Protocap and increasing sales of his standard products. The idea of reducing turnover shocked the MD. Meanwhile the Head Office in Birmingham wanted him to increase sales in Central and Eastern Europe.

He asked his Financial Controller to report on what more could be done to improve the financial situation and to reach the planned business targets.

This unit deals with:

a The language of instruction, impersonal decision-making, expressing purpose, talking about periods of time, giving advice, indirect speech and thought;

b The language of sales and profit forecasts, planning, production, management organisation for problem-solving.

The other serious problem for the Managing Director was Proteus's cash flow.

B Reading I

Extract from a Head Office Memorandum

From:	Group Export Manager, Proteus, Birmingham
To:	Managing Director, Proteus (Manara) Ltd
Subject:	The Protocap (Export Policy)
Date:	30th June 1995
Distribution:	Heads of all Proteus subsidiaries

1 At the last meeting of the Group Main Board it was decided that it should become a long-term aim to establish the Group as a worldwide supplier of public lighting systems.

2 The Protocap Energy Saver is a strategically important product. It should become the flagship product in the Proteus range and a major profit earner.

3 Subsidiary and associated companies should give top priority to formulating strategies to achieve these aims with a view to implementing plans by early 1997.

4 It has been decided that each company in the Group should plan to establish itself permanently in its area of responsibility ....

5 Proteus Manara should continue its successful penetration of the market in Central and Eastern Europe, by establishing a permanent presence there. The following options should be considered:

a. A substantial increase in the advertising budget
b. Setting up a subsidiary company
c. A joint venture
d. Appointing an exclusive or dedicated distributor ...

6 The financing of this expansion is already a problem. Borrowings are too high and banks in Manara are reluctant to lend more. It is a matter of the utmost urgency that solutions to these problems should be found with a view to pursuing the group objectives outlined above.

We look forward to hearing from you.

C Vocabulary

1 How are the following ideas expressed in the memorandum?

a) An official of the company who is in charge of exports of all the companies in the Proteus group
b) The chief officials of Proteus who oversee the management of all the companies in the group (*4 words, paragraph 1*)
c) ... supplier of lighting systems to the public sector (*5 words, paragraph 1*)
d) A manufactured item at the top of a list of other items made by one company (*7 words, paragraph 2*)
e) Central to all planning (*2 words, paragraph 2*)
f) Independent companies which co-operate but do not compete with us (*2 words, paragraph 3*)
g) Concentrate on this before anything else (*3 words, paragraph 3*)
h) Making plans of action (*6 words, paragraph 3*)
i) Carrying out prepared actions (*2 words, paragraph 3*)
j) Establishment of the sales of the products of a company in one country or region (*5 words, paragraph 5*)
k) Setting up in a country on a long-term basis (*4 words, paragraph 5*)
l) Think about these choices (*6 words, paragraph 5*)
m) Spending much more on publicity (*7 words, paragraph 5*)
n) A company set up by parties from different countries with equal interest (*2 words, paragraph 5*)
o) A sole agent in a country (*2 words, paragraph 5*)
p) An agent which sells the products of the principal and the products of no other company (*2 words, paragraph 5*)
q) Bank overdrafts (*1 word, paragraph 6*)
r) Unwilling but sympathetic (*1 word, paragraph 6*)
s) It is extremely important that this should be done before anything else. (*8 words, paragraph 6*)
t) There should be ways of overcoming these difficulties so that the overall aims of our companies, which we have already mentioned, can be achieved. (*17 words, paragraph 6*)

2 Decide on the best choice of word or phrase to complete each sentence.

a) Establishing a market in Manara should be a / *permanent objective* / *standing order* / *long-term aim* / *policy* / for the future.
b) It is important to / *settle* / *establish* / *strengthen* / *reinforce* / ourselves in the market.
c) They are major / *makers* / *providers* / *suppliers* / *sellers* / of building materials.
d) It will be necessary to set up a sales company if we want to / *get where we want* / *arrive at this target* / *achieve these aims.*
e) We should have a meeting / *in order to* / *with a view to* / *for the purpose of* / solving these problems.
f) It will be necessary to / *implement* / *carry out* / *do* / *make* / this plan in 1995.
g) By 1993 Proteus had / *fully developed* / *established a foothold in* / *penetrated* / the Barakonian market.
h) To set up in Barakonia, a / *very large* / *substantial* / *great* / *gigantic* / investment will be needed.

i) They / *gave the job to* / *appointed* / *handed the appointment to* / *bestowed responsibility on* / an experienced local company.

j) We are doing our best to find the / *solution to* / *answer to* / *escape from* / *way out from* / the problem.

3 Make appropriate noun phrases by joining words from the lists below. (The numbers in brackets show how many of the words on the left can be used with each noun.)

associated	venture (5)
exclusive	objectives (5)
dedicated	budget (5)
long-term	increase (4)
worldwide	range (2)
product	penetration (2)
subsidiary	supplier (4)
marketing	aim (4)
market	company (2)
substantial	distributor (3)
advertising	strategies (4)
joint	
group	

Synonyms

4 Match the words on the left with those of the same meaning on the right.

borrowing	think about (*vb*)
option	describe (*vb*)
aims	big (*adj*)
permanent (*adj*)	sole
establish	carry out (*vb*)
formulate	design
strategy	set up
implement (*vb*)	long-term (*adj*)
consider	choice
substantial (*adj*)	overdraft
exclusive	objectives
outline (*vb*)	plan of action

D Grammar

Instructions from above

Use of *should*

Look at how *should* is used in the memorandum on page 31.

A .... it *should become* a long-term aim ...
B It *should become* the main product ...
C Subsidiary and associated companies *should give* top priority ...
D .... each company in the group *should plan* ...
E Proteus Manara *should continue* its successful ...
F The following options *should be* considered...

1 Rewrite the following sentences as instructions.

a) Sales will be increased by 30 per cent.
b) You are the largest suppliers of paint in the North. (become)
c) You are planning to export to China.
d) Herbals aims to borrow up to £6,000,000 for expansion.

The impersonal passive

The following statement can be expressed in an impersonal way:

We have decided that it should become a long-term aim to establish the group as a worldwide supplier of public lighting systems.
It has been decided that it should become a long-term aim...

2 Make similar sentences from the table.

It has been decided that	a distributor sales it Proteus costs	should	be appointed in Zambia. be increased in Barakonia. become a long term aim... be established as a worldwide supplier... be reduced.

Can you make similar examples about the situation in your own organisation?

'Decided that' and 'decided to'

They decided to become worldwide suppliers of public lighting. (Proteus)

They decided *that Proteus should* become worldwide suppliers of public lighting.

3 Rewrite these sentences in the same way, using the prompts.

a) They decided to make it the main product in the Proteus range and a major profit earner. (the Protocap /become)
b) They decided to give top priority to formulating strategies to achieve these aims. (subsidiary and associated companies should)
c) They decided to make the Protocap Energy Saver a strategically important product. (should become)
d) They decided to implement the plans by early 1996. (the plans should be)
e) It has been decided to establish each company in the Group permanently in its area of responsibility. (each company in the .... should .... itself)
f) It has been decided to establish a permanent presence in Central and Eastern Europe. (Proteus Manara should ....)
g) It has been decided to consider the following options. (should be)

The following can be changed in the same way:

h) It is a matter of the utmost urgency to find solutions to these problems. (solutions .... should be ....)
i) It is extremely important to understand the financial health of a company before investing in it. (one should)

4 Choose the right preposition.

a) Proteus aims at penetration / *in* / *of* / *to* / *through* the market by the Protocap Energy Saver.
b) They must be prepared to finance an increase / *in* / *of* / *for* / *over* their advertising budget.
c) It may be necessary to set / *off* / *out* / *up* a subsidiary company.
d) They will seek further finance with a view / *to* / *of* / *for* / *in* pursuing the Group objectives outlined in the Chairman's report.
e) An increase / *of* / *with* / *by* / *in* sales is essential.

5 Make phrases like the example.

Example
A product which has strategic importance.
It is a strategically important product.

a) A forecast which was carefully calculated
b) A strategy which was thoughtfully formulated
c) A plan which was energetically implemented
d) A policy which was strongly supported
e) A presence which was permanently established

E Discussion

Ask and answer questions.

Who was the memorandum from?
Who was it sent to?
When was it written?

What was the memorandum about?
What else was it about?
What else?
What was decided at the Group Main Board?
What else was decided?
What long-term aim was stated?
What was decided about the Protocap?
What were subsidiaries and associated companies to do?
What was Proteus (Manara) to do?
What options for Proteus were suggested?
What were the problems for Proteus?
What was a matter of the utmost urgency?

F Reading II

The financial position of Proteus in July 1995

PROTEUS (MANARA) LIMITED

PROFIT AND LOSS STATEMENT

Six Months to June 30th 1995

('000 Manara dollars)

	1994 12 months Actual	*1995* 6 months Actual	*1995* 12 months Plan
SALES	2,400	1,455	3,500
COST OF SALES			
Opening inventory	250	350	150
Purchases	1,480	700	2,160
	1,730	1,050	2,310
Closing inventory	350	220	375
	1,380	830	1,935
Labour costs	245	135	350
Factory overheads	125	80	150
Total cost of sales	1,750	1,045	2,435
GROSS PROFIT	650	410	1,065
% of sales	27%	28%	30%
OPERATING EXPENSES			
Selling	440	250	500
Administration	160	95	180
Interest costs	30	12	15
Total operating expenses	630	357	695
PROFIT BEFORE TAX	20	53	370
TAXATION @ 40%	8	21	148
NET PROFIT	12	32	222
Net profit as % of sales	0.5	2.2	6.3

Sales and profit forecast 1995-6

PROTEUS (MANARA) LIMITED

PROTOCAP ENERGY SAVER

SALES AND PROFIT FORECAST 1995 - 6

('000 Manara dollars)

	1994 Full Year Actual	1995 6 months Actual	1995 Full Year Forecast	1996 Full Year Forecast
Sales volume forecast	700	566	1,200	1,400
List price	1,000	1,000	1,200	1,210
Sales discount (average percentage)	–	10%	–	2%
Average selling price	1,000	990	1,100	1,186
Sales value	700	560	1,320	1,660
Profit contribution	243	132	304	366
Percentage of sales	24%	12%	28%	30%

G Vocabulary

1 Choose the best explanation to show the meaning of each expression. Words are marked for stress, to help you with pronunciation.

a) **Fore**cast — i) plan ii) estimate iii) prediction iv) guess
b) **Dis**count — i) price reduction ii) low price iii) price increase iv) low cost
c) Contri**but**ion — i) increase ii) share iii) payment iv) yield

H Listing I

Dialogue I

Read the gapped dialogue below. Listen to the conversation on the cassette which practises the vocabulary introduced in the Profit and Loss Account (Reading I). Then complete the tapescript.

It is July 1995. The Financial Controller is again discussing the financial position of the company with the Managing Director. The Production Manager is also present. The Financial Controller speaks first.

FC ... so, overall the results of .... of 1995 are better than they were for the whole of 1994. Mind you, to make 2.2 per cent pre-tax profit on sales is .... and we are below the 1995 Plan.

MD Yes. That doesn't make it any better.

FC The .... is that the net profit for the twelve months of 1995 will be ...., better than the 1994 figure, but .... 1993. One good sign for the second six months is that .... are down.

MD So what are the main problem areas?

FC The main one is the .... of the Energy Saver, which is depressing profits. I must say that from a purely financial point of view, unless we can improve its sales and profit contribution, it would be better to consider discontinuing this product.

MD Well, you know what the answer is to that: it's the Proteus Group's policy to increase worldwide sales of the Energy Saver, so there's no question of dropping it.

As a matter of fact I've got a copy of the latest Head Office directive dealing with the Protocap. You can read it in your own office. You'll see that our main task is to boost sales volumes and values of the Protocap and reduce unit costs. On the other hand, I have already discussed the problem of increasing total sales value with the Marketing Manager. It's clear we can't raise prices because our competitors' prices are already 2 per cent below our price in most markets.

FC So our problem is how to boost sales and cut costs. Any problems in the production area?

I Vocabulary

Further practice

1 Complete the following sentences with words from Listening I.

a) The company's financial .... show lower net profits this year. *(1 word, lines 1-5)*
b) The weak .... is reflected in the turnover figure. *(1 word, lines 1-5)*
c) They listened to the weather .... on the radio. *(1 word, lines 5-10)*
d) Lower interest rates in Germany would have the effect of .... rates in other EC countries. *(1 word, lines 10-15)*
e) It will be necessary to .... marketing techniques if we are to increase sales. *(1 word, lines 10-15)*
f) Trades Union funds are made up of .... from members and income from investments. *(1 word, lines 10-15)*
g) The bus company has been gradually .... more and more services. *(1 word, lines 10-15)*
h) The Prime Minister may consider .... the Finance Minister during the Christmas break. *(1 word, lines 10-15)*
i) The Central Bank issues special .... to the commercial banks. *(1 word, lines 15-20)*
j) There are several ways of .... this problem. *(2 words, lines 15-20)*
k) The morale of the football team was .... by their club's supporters during the match. *(1 word, lines 15-20)*
l) The government constantly looks for ways to .... expenditure. *(1 word, lines 20-27)*

2 Make compound nouns by matching words on the left with appropriate words on the right.

financial	sales value
problem	directive
profit	sales
worldwide	costs
head office	areas
unit	contribution
total	

J Grammar

Sentence connectors

1 Note how the following are used to begin sentences. Can you match them with the words of similar meaning on the right?

So overall *(line 1)*	But against that is
Mind you, *(line 2)*	Therefore, what we have to do is
As a matter of fact, *(line 18)*	Actually, I
On the other hand, *(line 21)*	But you have to be careful
So our problem is ... *(line 26)*	Therefore, in general,

Can you make sentences of your own about your organisation's situation, beginning with the phrases on the left?

Talking about periods of time

2 Note how different parts of the year are referred to:

	Synonymous expressions
the first six months (*line 1*)	the second half of ....
the whole of 1994 (*line 2*)	-
the twelve months of 1995 (*line 6*)	the whole of ....
the figure for 1993 (*line 8*)	for the whole year
for the second six months (*lines 8-9*)	the second half of ....

Commenting

3 Study the example and complete the sentences.

Example
.... make 2 per cent pre-tax profit on sales .. a poor performance.
But, to make 2 per cent pre-tax profit on sales is a poor performance.

a) .... borrow money when interest rates are high ... expensive.
b) .... run up too big an inventory .... unwise.
c) .... have a profitable flagship product .... advantageous.

Reporting in the past

Indirect speech

4 Note that the Financial Controller made –

a) a definite statement about the present

'One good sign *is* that inventories *are* down.'
The FC said one good sign *was* that inventories *were* down.

b) a definite forecast about the future

'The latest forecast *is* that the net profit *will be* better.'
The FC said the latest forecast *was* that the net profit *would be* better.

Rewrite the following sentences in the past, beginning 'The Financial Controller said ....'.

a) The overall results of 1995 January – June are better than 1994.
b) It will be better to discontinue making this product.
c) Proteus will have to reduce turnover.

Expressing purpose

5 Complete these sentences, if possible from the point of view of your own organisation.

a) It is Proteus Group's policy to ....
It is (*name of your organisation*) policy to ....
b) You'll see that our main task is to ....

Denying possibility

6 Look at how the Managing Director rejects the Financial Controller's suggestion, and complete the sentences in the same way.

.... (drop) it.
So there's no question of dropping it.

a) .... (sell) the Lodz factory.
b) .... (open) the exhibition before the Queen arrives.
c) .... (return) to the bad old days.

Defining participles

Note how the *-ing* form of the verb can replace a defining relative clause.

I've got a copy of the directive *which deals* with the Protocap.
I've got a copy of the directive *dealing* with the Protocap.

This shows us which directive is being talked about.

7 Rewrite the following sentences in the same way.

a) Have you seen the Balance Sheet which shows the latest position?
b) Which are the operating costs which cause the most problems?
c) I'll show you some figures which prove my point.
d) There are several problems which need to be dealt with.

K Listening II

The Managing Director has just been talking about the directive from Head Office which says Proteus Manara should concentrate on the Protocap. The Financial Controller asks the Production Manager about his problems and they discuss various practical ways to implement the company policy of promoting the Protocap.

Words or phrases with the following meanings have been taken out of the tapescript. Read the list. Read the gapped tapescript. Then listen to the dialogue and complete the tapescript. Then write down the correct phrase from the tape to match each meaning.

a) A complete set of actions of factory machinery needed to produce one finished product (*2 words*)
b) Taking up a great deal of time (*2 words*)
c) The cost of making one product in a factory (*2 words*)
d) The time needed to make machines in a factory ready to start work (*3 words*)
e) The cost, aimed at by the management, of producing one product (*4 words*)
f) To arrange the manufacturing process in a factory in a different way (*4 words*)
g) The speed of production measured in the number of units made in an hour (*2 words*)
h) To make it helpfully cheap (*4 words*)
i) A difficult thing to do (*3 words* – a colloquial expression)

j) Put money into a business (*1 word*)
k) A hard selling effort into publicising a product with a view to selling it (*3 words*)
l) A price reduction depending on how many are bought (*2 words*)

Use of vocabulary: Dialogue 2

FC – .... how to boost sales and cut costs. Any problems in the production area?

PM Yes, quite serious ones, caused by short (1).......... .... on the Protocap. A lot of time is spent setting up each run. Also the planning and administration for each run is very (2).......... .... and expensive.

MD Yes, I am aware of that, but there's little we can do in the short term except go for higher sales volumes. What are the financial effects of doing this?

FC The (3).......... .... of production are 20 per cent above plan. This is because production runs have to be charged with labour and overhead on the basis of total time spent in the factory. This includes (4).......... .... – and so we are always (5) ....

PM One way to reduce costs is to use other materials for the Protocap. I could also (6).................... .... to increase the (7).................... .... But to get (8).................... .... we'd need to double the number we produce.

MD That's (9)...... .... However, Head Office engineering staff have already made some suggestions for technical improvements. They are coming over here from the UK next week to discuss them.

What I really want to do is to reduce the cost of the Energy Saver, hold its selling price or even reduce it by 5 per cent. We could (10).................... say $50,000 in an (11).................... .... and offer customers (12).......... ....

L Listening III

1 Again, words or phrases with the following meanings have been taken out of the tapescript. Read the list. Read the skeleton tapescript. Listen to the dialogue and complete the tapescript. Then write down the correct phrase from the tape to match each meaning.

a) To succeed in making the amount of net profit we aim to make (*6 words*)
b) A prediction of the amount we are going to sell of each product and the amount we are going to sell in each geographical area (*8 words*)
c) Putting all our effort into (*2 words*)
d) The cheapest way of getting the job done properly (*5 words*)
e) A group of people organised to do a certain job (*2 words*)
f) To design a procedure to increase the size of the company (*6 words*)
g) Job description (*3 words*)

Use of vocabulary: Dialogue 3

2 The Managing Director says what he wants the Financial Controller, Production Manager and the Marketing Manager to do.

MD We must see what extra turnover we need, (1).......... .... and then decide how to get those extra sales.

FC I'll need a (2).................... .... with expected selling prices and selling costs.

MD I'll get together with the Marketing Manager and produce the figures you need. It'll take a day or two. Meanwhile I want the two of you to produce a plan for cost reductions on the Energy Saver and show me the possible effects on the company's net profit.

Gentlemen, the principal task is to boost the Protocap sales, and we'll achieve that by (3).................... .... our overseas markets. So we must find (4)...... .... of strengthening our position in Central and Eastern Europe.

I'm setting up a (5) .... (6) .... It will (7)............... ..... you two and the Marketing Manager. I'll draft some (8) .... for you tomorrow and let Head Office know of our intentions.

UNIT 4 Doubtful Ratios

A Introduction

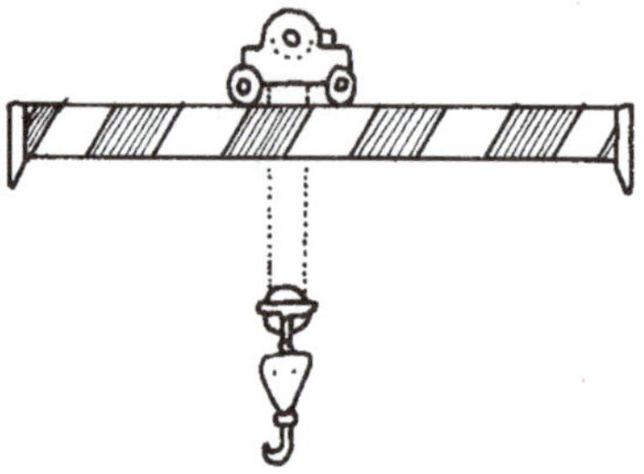

The story so far

The Managing Director and Financial Controller of Proteus Manara Ltd have decided that the chief cause of their troubles is their main product - the Protocap, an electrical energy saver. Its gross profit margin fell from 31 per cent of sales in 1993 to 14 per cent in 1994, as a result of price cutting. The Financial Controller then advised the Managing Director to cut sales of the Protocap and concentrate on other products.

But then a Head Office directive said that the Protocap was to be the flagship product of the Group. It should be distributed all over the world. The Manara Managing Director replied that he would be proposing a plan for expanding sales of the Protocap within three weeks.

At the same time, several aspects of the Protocap needed to be corrected: competition was preventing an increase of the selling price; short production runs were causing planning problems in the factory and were keeping unit costs high; there was not enough detailed information in the costing records; and bad management of inventories and customer receivables was reducing cash flow and increasing financial costs.

The Managing Director of Proteus Manara has already set up a task force of senior managers to produce a plan to restore profits.

Contents of this unit:

a Profit and Loss ratios
b Balance Sheet ratios
c Balance Sheet analysis

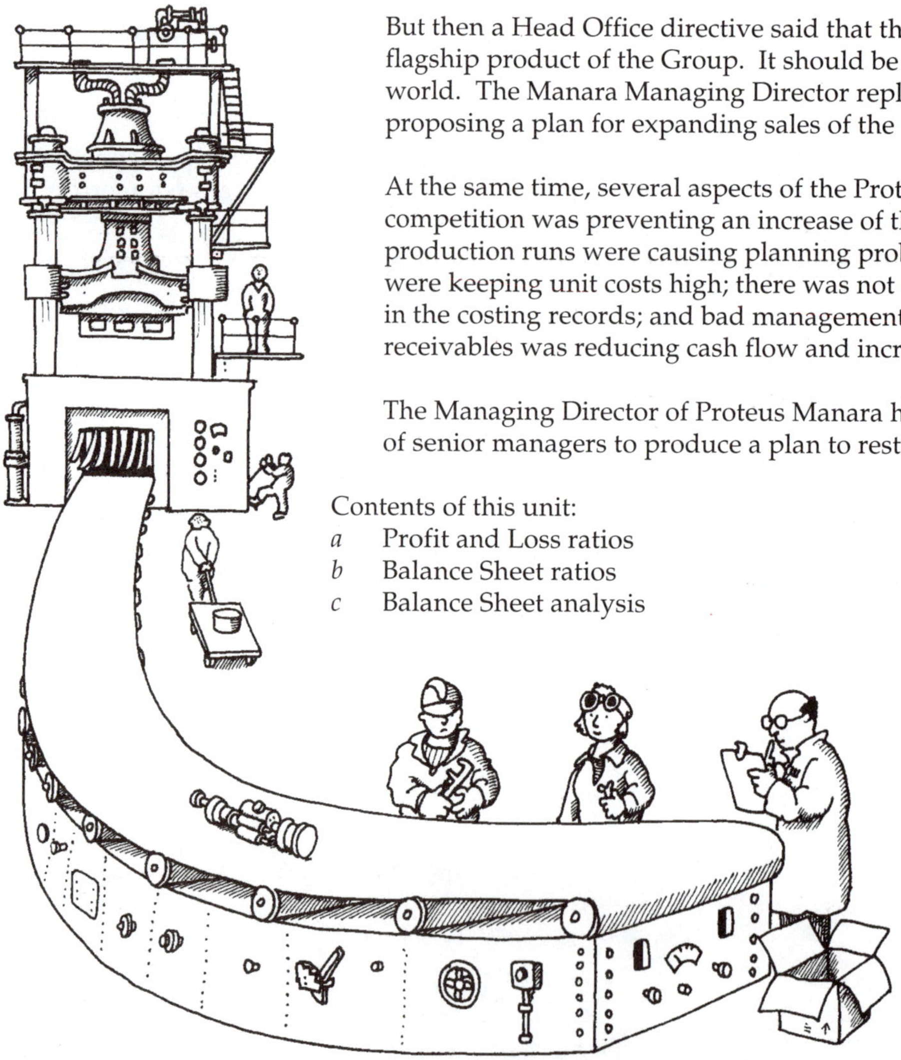

Short production runs were causing planning problems in the factory...

B Reading I

In July 1995 the Head Office finance department asked the Financial Controller of Proteus Manara to explain the company's accounting problems. An extract from this Memorandum is given below.

'.......... we are concerned at some of the accounting ratios you have reported. It is important to solve these problems before you go ahead with any expansion project.

PROFIT AND LOSS RATIOS

Material costs – the 1995 Plan says these should be reduced to 55 per cent of sales. So far in 1995, the ratio is 42 per cent which does not look right and needs further explanation.

Factory overheads – This should have been reduced in 1995 to 4 per cent of sales. In fact it is slightly up on the 1994 figure.

Gross profit – You are 10 percentage points below Plan. To what extent does this represent a reduction in selling prices or sales discounting, and to what extent is it due to increases in cost?

Selling and administrative expenses – For the year to date both ratios are below Plan and in line with Plan in dollars. What is your forecast for the full year 1995 and what steps will be taken to control these expenses?

BALANCE SHEET RATIOS

Receivables – Your figure is over Plan and beyond the Group's average of 45 days. Please explain the causes and explain how you intend to reduce this figure.

Inventory – Based on actual data for 1995, we calculate your current inventory stands at 84 days' consumption, while your 1995 Plan figure should be 32 days. What is the forecast for inventory levels for the rest of 1995?'

C Vocabulary

1 Match each of these expressions with examples a) – j).

Selling and administrative expenses   accounting ratios   ratios
receivables   material costs   factory overheads   consumption
balance sheet items   inventory   forecasts

a) Kilometres per hour; revolutions per minute; price earnings
b) Tomorrow the weather will be dry; they will complete the building in two months' time; conditions will improve next year
c) Copper wire: $350 a tonne; Sheet metal: $40; Plastic: £120 a tonne
d) Eating; drinking; using oil; burning coal; using materials to manufacture things
e) overheads to sales; profit to capital employed; material cost per unit
f) Receivables; inventory
g) 32 tonnes fuel oil; 50 tonnes copper wire; 5 tonnes sheet metal; 4.5 tonnes polyethylene
h) power; rent; building maintenance; cleaning
i) salaries of salespeople; salaries of office staff; office heating; stationery; advertising
j) Unpaid invoices; debtors

2 How are the following ideas expressed in the reading passage?

a) Worried about (*2 words, paragraph 1*)
b) Given in a financial document (*1 word, paragraph 1*)
c) A little higher than, somewhat more than (*3 words, paragraph 3*)
d) Money remaining from sales before deducting operating costs (*2 words, paragraph 4*)
e) Not in accordance with the scheme of the Group (*2 words, paragraph 5*)
f) Offering special price reductions to buyers (*8 words, paragraph 4*)
g) All the time this year until now (*5 words, paragraph 5*)
h) In accordance with the scheme of the group (*4 words, paragraph 5*)
i) List of items in store (*1 word, paragraph 7*)

Less formal to more formal

3 Choose expressions from the box to replace the words in italics.

steps will be taken	indicate	reported	concerned at	
current inventory	requires	intend	analysis	proceed

a) We are *worried about* some of the accounting ratios you have told us about.
b) It is important to solve these problems before you *go ahead* with any expansion project.
c) Material Costs – the 1995 Plan *says* that these should be reduced to 55 per cent of sales.
d) So far in 1995, the ratio is 42 per cent; which does not look right and needs further *investigation*.
e) Gross profit – You are 10 percentage points below Plan. To what extent does this *show* a reduction in selling prices or sales discounting, and to what extent is it due to increases in cost?
f) What is your forecast for the full year 1995 and what *are you going to do* to control these expenses?
g) Receivables – Your figure is over Plan and beyond the Group's average of 45 days. Please explain the causes and how you *are going* to reduce this figure.
h) Based on actual data for 1995, we calculate your *present stock* stands at 84 days' consumption.

D Grammar

Admonishing or prescribing

1 This is language generally used by superiors to subordinates, and is a mixture of telling and advising.

Examples

A It is important to solve these problems before you go ahead with any expansion project.

Pattern: *it is* + adjective + infinitive + predicate

B .... these should be reduced to 42 per cent of sales

C This should have been reduced in 1995 to 4 per cent of sales.

D .... your 1995 Plan figure should be 32 days.

Pattern: Subject + *should* + verb + predicate

The first example can be rewritten using *should*:

It is important to solve these problems before you go ahead.
These problems should be solved before you go ahead.

2 Rewrite the sentences below in the same way.

a) It is important to reduce raw materials to 42 per cent of sales.
b) It is important to make sure these ratios follow the Plan.
c) It is vital to reduce the average to 32 days.
d) It is a matter of urgency to bring factory overheads down to 4 per cent of sales.

3 Now rewrite the following sentences, beginning with *It is* ... . Use the notes to help you.

Example

These should be reduced to 42 per cent of sales.
It is important to reduce these to 42 per cent of sales.

a) A product development plan should be produced before visiting Warsaw. (It is vital to ....)
b) The balance sheet ratios should be examined as soon as possible. (It is of the utmost importance to ....)
c) The finances of Proteus Manara should be put on a firm basis before expanding overseas. (It is important to ....)
d) The costing system should be looked at first of all. (It is essential to ....)
e) The Managing Director should go over the finances carefully with the Financial Controller before coming to Birmingham. (It would be useful for the .... to ....)
f) The Production Manager should work out a plan to reduce inventory levels. (It is crucial for .... to ....)

Determiners

4 The 'Story so far' at the beginning of the unit is given below, showing the determiner of each noun phrase:

Determiner **Noun phrase**	**Explanation**
The Managing Director and	One particular Managing Director in the mind of the writer.
Financial Controller of	'The' at the beginning of the sentence has this meaning.
Proteus (Manara) Ltd have decided	name (normally no determiner)
the chief cause of	One particular cause
their troubles is	Whose troubles?
their main product –	Whose main product?
the Protocap	The one and only Protocap
an electrical energy saver.	Only one among others
Its gross profit margin fell from 31 per cent of	The profit margin of what?
sales in 1993 to 14 per cent in 1994, as	Zero determiner or *the* is optional here
a result of price cutting.	only one result among others
The Financial Controller then advised	The Financial Controller of Proteus Manara
the Managing Director to cut	
sales of	Zero det./ *the* optional
the Protocap and concentrate on	The one and only Protocap
other products.	'other' = any other

5 Now try assigning rules to the use of the determiners in italics below.

But then

a) *a* Head Office directive said the Protocap was to be
b) *the* flagship product of the Group. It should be distributed all over
c) *the* world. The Manara Managing Director replied that he would be proposing
d) *a* plan for expanding
e) sales of the Protocap within (zero determiner)
f) three weeks. (zero determiner)
g) at *the* same time,
h) *several* aspects of the Protocap needed to be corrected:
i) competition was preventing (zero determiner)
j) *an* increase in the selling price;
k) short production runs were causing (zero determiner)
l) planning problems in the factory and were keeping unit costs high. (zero determiner)

E Listening I

Return on capital

The Managing Director of Proteus Manara has to attend a meeting at Head Office and explain his poor financial figures to the Group Chairman. So he needs to understand not only the ratios used by his accountants, but also the adverse ratios in the balance sheet. Listen to the tape and complete the tapescript. (*Note*: Some spaces have more than one word).

MD By the way, next week I've got the Group Meeting in Birmingham, so perhaps you could go over the (1) .... ratios to make sure I am clear on what they mean!

FC OK, let's begin with the (2) .... – our return on capital. Although it only summarises our (3) ...., this ratio and the (4).................... are the ones which most interest the (5).................... and affect the Group (6)....................

MD If I understand it correctly, we take profit as a (7).................... of capital employed –

FC Yes, but don't forget, it's profit after tax, and we usually (8).................... profit in relation to the (9).................................... during the year. That's because our profit is earned (10).................... the year.

MD By 'net' you mean after deducting all (11)....................?

FC That's right.

MD So if our profit in 1994 was (12)........... and our average capital employed was about (13)...................., our return on capital was, let's see, 1.5 per cent!! That can't be right. It's ridiculously low! Interest rates last year (14).................... 8-9 per cent. Then there's (15).................... And wasn't our return on capital in 1990 about 12 or 13 per cent?

FC Yes that's true. But to be fair, a low return on capital was (16).................. in the 1994 (17)...................., because of our heavy investment in the Protocap Energy Saver.

MD Yes, but not 1.5 per cent! Which is why for us it's a case of (18)....................! We should have been properly financed when we were (19).................... here in Manara. The Group have always preferred us to obtain our own finance once they'd (20).................... their $500,000 of (21)..................

FC We did ask for additional support, but at the time they said the (22).................... was too great and they preferred us to borrow in Manara dollars even if (23).................... interest rates were higher than in the UK. They accepted a lower return on capital.

(*Note*: You may wish to find out more about words used in the dialogue, which may be dealt with in more detail in earlier units. You can look up these words in the Index.)

F Vocabulary

Equivalent words and phrases

1 How are the following ideas expressed in the dialogue?

a) unfavourable
b) the people who have invested money in the company
c) the money paid out each year to the people who have invested money in the company
d) debts
e) putting a lot of money into
f) grow bigger or go bankrupt

2 Match the expressions from the dialogue on the left with the correct explanations on the right.

can't be right	wanted
express profit	putting a large amount of capital into
only summarises	make the company bigger or go down
heavy investment in	received enough investment
expand or bust	simply draws conclusions about
properly financed	give the figure of
preferred to	must be wrong

3 What are the following examples of?

a) kilometres per hour (kph); revolutions per minute (rpm)
b) 50 per cent drop in exam success rates; a fall in earnings per share; increase in consumption of litres per kilometre by your car
c) the return on capital
d) debts, tax, electricity bill, telephone bill, money borrowed from the bank
e) 8 per cent, 8.5 per cent, 9 per cent

4 Use these verbs from Listening I to complete the sentences.

affect	express	employ	foresee	establish	prefer

a) Can you .... any problems with next week's work?
b) What can you .... about the damage?
c) With such a low return, the money would be better .... somewhere else.
d) I would .... you to ring me during office hours.
e) A price rise will .... sales badly.
f) Interest rates are usually .... as percentage rates per year.

G Discussion

Working with a partner, ask and answer these questions on Listening I.

a) Why does the Proteus Managing Director need to understand the meaning of all the ratios used by the 'finance people'?
b) What will the Proteus Managing Director have to explain to the Chairman of the Group?
c) Which is the key ratio, according to the Financial Controller?
d) Which ratios are of most interest to shareholders, according to the Financial Controller?
e) Expand this definition:
The return on capital is calculated as profits as a percentage of capital employed.
f) Why was there a low return on capital in 1994?
g) Why did the Proteus Group not invest more than $500,000 in their Manara subsidiary when it was first set up?

H Listening II

Customer receivables

The Financial Controller and the Managing Director continue their conversation. Listen carefully for the phrases used by the speakers to connect their speech. These phrases connect with what has gone before and lead in to what they are going to say.

1 Listen to the tape and complete the tapescript.
(*Note*: Some spaces have more than one word.)

MD (1)........., (2)......... look at customer receivables. How can I explain (3)......... to the Chairman?

FC Group procedures express (4)......... as days of sales to make (5)......... comparable with other years and with other companies of (6)......... Group.

(7)......... if in December 1994, our receivables were $550,000 and our sales for the year were $2.4 million, (8)......... we assume there are 240 working days in a year ((9)......... procedure requires) the average sales were $10,000 per day.

MD (10)......... (11)......... that means $550,000 worth of receivables divided by one day of sales or $10,000 gives an average of 55. That's days of sales. So if our normal credit terms are 30 days, (12)......... are getting 25 days free finance from us! What was the ratio for 1993?

FC (13)......... – sales of 2 million - that's $8,333 per day and receivables were $420,000 which, divided by $8,333, (14)......... 50.4 days.

MD (15)......... wasn't a satisfactory ratio. What's the average for the Group?

FC It's difficult (16).......... .... between different countries but I believe that 40-45 days would be acceptable.

MD (17).........., we're still ten days too high. You're responsible for credit control, (18).......... you could you let me have an action plan to get (19).......... down to 45 days by the end of the year (20).......... .... inventories[...]

I Vocabulary

How are the following ideas expressed in Listening II?

a) Unpaid invoices (*2 words*)
b) Rules laid down by the Proteus companies (*2 words*)
c) Explain (*1 word*)
d) To give a uniform method of comparison between (*5 words*)
e) Monday, Tuesday, Wednesday, Thursday, Friday (*2 words*)
f) The usual period of time we allow customers to pay for goods (*4 words*)
g) An interest-free loan (*2 words*)
h) Acceptable (*1 word*)
i) Thought good (*2 words*)
j) Reduce this amount to (*5 words*)

J Grammar

Suggesting immediate action

Let's + verb is often used to suggest immediate action.

Example
Let's look at customer receivables.

1 Make your own suggestions, using the notes below.

a) look at the inventories
b) go over the balance sheet ratios
c) deal with the costing problems next
d) put this into our expansion plan

Allowing thinking time

Let's + verb is one of several formulae used to give thinking time.

Examples
Let's see - sales of 2 million - that's . . . .
Let me think.
Just a moment.
Hang on a minute.

2 Use the examples with the notes below to make your own sentences.

a) In December 1994, our receivables were $550,000 and our sales for the year were $2.4 million.
b) That's 55 days of sales.
c) If our normal credit terms are 30 days, the customers are getting 25 days free finance from us!

Verbs: express, give, show

Example
Group procedures *express* receivables *as* days of sales
Turnover *is expressed in* money terms
Sales *are expressed in* dollars.

3 Use the verbs *express, give* or *show* to complete the sentences.

a) The value of the contract .... Deutschmarks. (*give*)
b) Raw materials .... in the balance sheet .... part of the inventory. (*show*)
c) Money owed to the bank .... a liability.
d) The total value of production ....
e) Volume of sales .... metric tonnes.
f) Consumption of fuel .... litres.

The simple past conditional: If A was true then B was true

Example
If in December 1991, our receivables *were* $550,000 and our sales for the year *were* $2.4 million, and if we *assume* there are 240 working days in a year, the average sales *were* $10,000 per day.

4 What tenses are used in the above example?

a) If the road .... (be) .... blocked, there ....(be).......... no other way out.
b) If sales ...(be) ... $8,333 per day and receivables ....(be)......... $420 thousand we ... (have) ... 50.4 days of sales.

Simple present conditional: If A is true then B is true

Example
So if our normal credit terms *are* 30 days, these people *are getting* 25 days free finance from us!

This is almost the same as the conditional explained in 4 above. But this time both clauses have verbs in the present tense.

Text grammar: Connecting phrases

5 Go through the connecting phrases you wrote down while listening to the tape and say which ones are used to express the following:

a) Result or consequence
b) Referring to something or someone outside the text
c) Referring back to the speaker and listener
d) Rejection
e) Referring back to what has just been said
f) Maintaining a point
g) Referring back to what has been discussed using another phrase
h) Attention-getting
i) The speaker tells the listeners what to do or what they are going to do next
j) Referring to a person or thing well known to both listener and speaker
k) Referring back to something just mentioned
l) Comparing
m) Understanding and agreeing

K Game

Aim: to practise saying, spelling and defining the accountancy terms and expressions learnt so far.

There is a list of terms on the following page. Write them on separate cards or pieces of paper.
Deal out the cards face down to the group. Everybody should try and collect as many cards as possible by asking for them, within a fixed time of (say) 15 minutes. The winner is the one who has most cards when the time is up.

A Excuse me, have you got 'Return on capital'?
B Can you spell it?
A Yes ....
B Here you are.

If A makes a mistake in spelling, then B keeps the card.

A more difficult version would be for B to ask A to give a good definition of the expression *without* looking it up in the glossary.

List of terms

Accounting ratio
Adverse ratios
Average net capital
Action plan
Balance Sheet ratios
Balance Sheet analysis
Competition
Costing records
Customer receivables
Cash flow
Creditors
Chairman
Credit control
Directive
Dividend
Days of sales
Earnings per share
Exchange risk
Financial Controller
Flagship product
Financial costs
Factory overheads
Forecast
Free finance
Gross profit margin
Group
Gross profit
Inventories
Investment
Inflation
Invoices
Key ratio
Liabilities
Local interest rates
Material costs
Memorandum
Price cutting
Production runs
Profit and Loss ratios
Present stock
Profitability
Percentage
Return on capital
Selling price
Sales discounting
Selling and administrative expenses
Shareholders
Share capital
Task force
Unit costs

UNIT 5

The Way Forward

A Introduction

The story so far

Another memorandum from Head Office criticised Proteus's accounting ratios in the Balance Sheet and Profit and Loss account. The Managing Director of Proteus Manara was told that he must answer the questions they raised, and solve any problems arising from them, before going ahead with any scheme for expansion of export markets.

The Financial Controller spent time explaining the ratios to the Managing Director. He would then have a clear understanding of the financial situation when he attended the quarterly meeting of heads of subsidiaries in Birmingham.

Meanwhile the Proteus management team in Manara were working on the plan for expansion. One of their main concerns was to reduce the cost of the Protocap Energy Saver - the most important product. So the Financial Controller started work on the costing system, the Production Manager on re-organising the assembly line and using alternative materials, and the Marketing Manager on possibilities of expanding into Central and Eastern Europe.

This unit contains:

a A directive from the Proteus Head Office to its Manara subsidiary
b A Head Office memo expressing concern about the subsidiary
c The Financial Controller's explanation of Activity Costing.

The Financial Controller spent time explaining the ratios to the Managing Director.

B Reading I

1 The Financial Controller said earlier (Unit 2, Listening II, p.24) that Proteus should reduce sales of the Protocap and increase sales of other more profitable products. This advise goes against Group policy, which requires sales of the Protocap to be boosted.

a) Is this a deadlock situation?
b) How can it be resolved?
c) What would you do if you were the Managing Director of Proteus Manara?

A directive from Head Office (Unit 3, p. 31) stated as Group policy that the Protocap was to become the flagship product of the Group and sales should be increased.

Another memorandum from Head Office (p. 45) pointed out several weaknesses in the Proteus Manara Balance Sheet and Profit and Loss Account.

Memorandum from the Managing Director Proteus (Manara) Ltd
Date: 12th July

To:
Marketing Manager Ref: MD1401/fhd
Financial Controller
Production Manager

Copies to:
Product Development
Personnel & Training
Head Office,
Operations & Finance

Subject: MANARA EXPANSION TASK FORCE

INTRODUCTION

.... Proteus Manara will not be able to reach its target return on capital from sales in the EU, due to intense domestic competition and low margins. This leaves the development of export markets as a possible way forward.

At the same time, other subsidiaries of the group are in good positions to develop markets in the rest of the world. So it is clear that Proteus Manara should concentrate on Central and Eastern Europe.

TERMS OF REFERENCE

	Responsibilities
Financial Controller	Review all aspects of costing and preparation of financial documents of the project
Production Manager	Manufacturing and procurement
Marketing Manager	Market and product development

The task force should carry out desk research to obtain information on markets, business conditions and competitors. They should report back to me within 21 days with marketing and financial targets.

C Vocabulary

2 Now read the extract below.

1 Choose the best alternative to complete the sentences.

a) They decided to export because of strong / *home* / *domestic* / *national* / *local* competition.
b) They had to / *develop* / *build up* / *establish* / *locate* other markets where they could sell the Protocap.
c) They were unable to / *arrive at* / *succeed* / *reach* / *come to* their target for return on capital.
d) The Managing Director asked his team to / *carry out* / *do* / *make* / *undertake* desk research.
e) Head Office agreed that Proteus Manara should / *concentrate on* / *take over* / *take on* / *stay on* Eastern Europe.
f) They decided to / *revise* / *look over* / *examine* / *review* the costing system.
g) The Marketing Manager would have to / *locate* / *obtain* / *become* / *invent* as much information as possible about the market in Barakonia.
h) He asked them to / *report back* / *let him know* / *advise* / *review* in two weeks' time.

2 Choose words or phrases from the list on the right which come closest to the meaning of the words from Reading I listed on the left.

a) directive	request, order, suggestion, advice
b) terms of reference	structure, system, framework, unit
c) the EU	The Common Market, export conditions, European Union, European Commission
d) costing	calculating the cost, analysis of costs, working out how much to invest.
e) procurement	hiring for use, finding and buying, preparing for production

3 Use phrases from the box to complete the paragraph.

product development desk research marketing targets financial targets

Before exporting to a country or even visiting it, Proteus will carry out as much .... as possible. The purpose is to establish as many facts and collect as much information as possible before spending the money on an expensive visit. It will then be possible to decide on .... which will show which products are to be sold in which areas and at what price. Then the accountant will set the .... from the projected sales figures and costs. Meanwhile the production department will continue to be concerned with .... to ensure that the Protocap is modified, if necessary, to meet the needs of the market.

D Grammar

Reported directives and recommendations

Examples

A The Financial Controller said that Proteus should reduce sales of the Protocap.

B A directive from Head Office stated that the Protocap was to become the flagship product of the group.

Should is used for a recommendation or suggestion, while *is to, am to, are to* are used for directives.

1 Complete the following with *should* or *is to, am to, are to.*

a) The accountant said we .... make more profit.
b) The boss said I .... work harder.
c) She said we .... not reduce the selling price.
d) The manager told them they .... increase sales.
e) The policeman said I .... pay a $500 fine.
f) The report concluded that Proteus .... set up a joint venture subsidiary in Central Europe.

Impersonal sentences

Example

It is appreciated that no action can be taken at present.

2 Can you make sentences of your own starting in the same way? Use the notes below and choose a suitable tense for the verb.

a) (Demonstrate) that close relations (establish) with ....
b) (suspect) that there (be) some corruption in the government.
c) (Fear) that prices (go up) this winter.
d) (Think) that most people (not like) to live alone.
e) (Prove) that some athletes (take) drugs.
f) (Know) that the sun (rise) tomorrow.

Looking for rules

Determiners

3 Determiners are words such as *the, a, an, this, that, these* and *those* which come before nouns or noun phrases. *The* and *a* are determiners known as the **definite** and **indefinite article**. There is also a silent or invisible one known as **zero determiner** which is very important. Compare

Analysis of the balance sheet
with
Balance sheet analysis

The first one refers to a particular balance sheet the speaker or writer has in mind, while the second refers to the general activity of analysing balance sheets. In this way, zero determiner carries important meaning.

Look at more examples of nouns and noun phrases from Reading 1:

Noun phrase	*Type of determiner*
The Financial Controller said that	definite article
Proteus should reduce	zero determiner
sales of	zero determiner
the Protocap and increase sales of	definite article
other more profitable products.	indefinite determiner
This advice goes against	demonstrative determiner
Group policy which wants	zero determiner
sales of	zero determiner
the Protocap to be boosted.	definite article

Rules: There are three kinds of rule, which may begin like this:

You must use a determiner if you are referring to ....
You may, if you like, use a determiner if ....
You must not use a determiner if you are referring to ....

Can you say why determiners are used or not used in the above examples? Look at some explanations:

– a deadlock situation
  The writer must use the indefinite article here because he is referring to no particular situation.

– the Managing Director of Proteus
  The writer must use the definite article here because he is referring to one unique Managing Director.

– turning to the East
  There is only one area called 'the East' so it is unique and *the* must be used here. If you say 'They turned east', you are referring to the general direction east, and not to a specific place.

A general rule: The English determiner system is used to show the degree of particularity or specificity which must be shown for every noun or noun phrase.

4 Try to explain the determiners in the following extracts from the resumé on page 57 and from Reading I.

a) A directive from
b) Head Office stated that it was
c) Group policy that
d) the Protocap was to become
e) the flagship product of
f) the Group and
g) sales should be increased.
h) Proteus Manara will not be able to reach
i) its target return on capital from
j) the EC, due to
k) domestic competition and
l) low margins. This leaves ...

E Discussion

Question forms

Ask and answer these questions with a partner. (The question forms are arranged in order of events at Proteus.)

	was the chief cause of Proteus's troubles?
	is the Proteus flagship product?
What	was the gross profit margin in 1993?
	was the gross profit margin in 1994?
	was the directive from Head Office about?

Why did the gross profit margin fall in 1994?

What aspects of the Protocap needed to be corrected?
What other aspects needed to be corrected?
What else?
Anything else?

	preventing an increase of the selling price?
	the cause of planning problems in the factory?
What was	keeping unit costs high?
	reducing cash flow?
	increasing financial costs?

What did Head Office in Birmingham say about the Protocap?
What else did it say?
Anything else?

What has the Managing Director asked his managers to do?

How did the advice of the Financial Controller go against Group policy?
Why will Proteus not be able to reach its target return on capital from sales in the EC?
Why was the development of other export markets looked on as a possible solution to the problem?
Why should Proteus Manara concentrate on Central and Eastern Europe?
What did the Managing Director set up a task force to do?
Who was in the task force?
What were their responsibilities?
How much time did he give them for their task?

F Reading II

(This memo arrived soon after the Proteus Managing Director returned from the quarterly meeting at Birmingham)

From: the Group Managing Director
To: the Managing Director, Proteus Manara

QUARTERLY MANAGEMENT MEETING

The Chairman and I are very interested in the prospects which you described for the Group in Central and Eastern Europe, and look forward to receiving a detailed plan.

However we are worried about the dangerous financial position of Proteus Manara because of the large fall in net profit, the increase in your local borrowings and the fall of value of the Manara Dollar in the foreign exchange markets.

I understand the advantage of borrowing in local currencies, but this may be offset by the loss of profits when converted into Sterling.

We are also still waiting for the Manara and British governments to sign a double taxation treaty. Until then the double taxation of profits from Manara may reduce the Group's earnings per share.

Fortunately this is not a serious problem at present because your net profit is so low. However, if your expansion project succeeds, the conversion into Sterling of the greater net profit may increase difficulties.

Please instruct your Financial Controller to discuss these matters in detail with Head Office Finance Department. He should also make some comments in the 1995 profit forecast which is due in October when we begin to prepare the 1996 budget.

Both the Chairman and I would like to hear how you propose to overcome the problems of your gross profit levels, financial structure and working capital.

G Vocabulary

1 Find expressions which could be replaced by the following:

a) .... I must express our concern .... (*4 words, paragraph 2*)
b) .... in view of the substantial .... (*4 words, paragraph 2*)
c) .... deterioration .... (*1 word, paragraph 2*)
d) .... appreciate the benefit .... (*3 words, paragraph 3*)
e) .... adversely affect .... (*1 word, paragraph 4*)
f) .... achieves its objectives .... (*1 word, paragraph 5*)
g) .... changing .... into pounds .... (*1 word, paragraph 5*)

2 Use the words below to complete the sentences.

Nouns:
prospects, local borrowings, earnings per share
(*Note that the above nouns are usually in the plural.*)
foreign exchange, double taxation, working capital
(*Note that the above nouns occur only in the singular.*)
budget, local currency

Verbs: offset, convert

a) He .... his travelling expenses against income tax.
b) If the group's subsidiaries needed extra capital they were not allowed to go to the international markets but had to rely on ....
c) With so much money tied up in their inventory, the company was suffering from a shortage of ....
d) The pound gained 2 points in the .... markets.
e) The .... of the business were good, so he looked forward to a bright future.
f) She was afraid of a devaluation of the Forint and so .... all her spare cash into Deutschmarks.
g) Monthly payments for the car made a big hole in their spending ....
h) Every time he crossed a frontier he changed all his money into the ....
i) Since they needed income rather than capital growth, they bought securities which promised good ....
j) A .... situation is when the host country taxes profits of a foreign subsidiary which are taxed again after they have been paid into the country of the parent company.

Use of prepositions

3 Complete the sentences with the best choice of preposition.

Type A: *be* + adjective + preposition
a) We would be interested / *with* / *for* / *in* / your plans.
b) We are worried / *about* / *for* / *at* / the dangerous financial position of Proteus Manara.

Type B: verb + preposition

c) We are waiting / *a change* / *to change* / *for a change* / in the law.
d) We ought to discuss these matters / *in* / *for* / *with* / the Chief Accountant.
e) They thought it better to borrow / *from* / *in* / *by* / *with* / local banks.
f) They thought it better to borrow / *from* / *in* / *by* / *with* / local currencies.

Type C: noun + preposition

g) The Chairman understood the advantage / *for* / *of* / *in* / locally financed projects.
h) There may be a large fall / *with* / *of* / *in* / net profit.
i) The increase / *by* / *of* / *in* / your local borrowings is too fast.

H Grammar

Logical connectors

1 Find the expressions in italics in Reading II and say which sort of logical connection they make with what has gone before in the text: addition, sequencing, contrast or reason.

a) *However*
b) *but* this may be offset
c) We are *also* still waiting for
d) *Until then* the double taxation of profits from Manara may reduce the Group's earnings per share.
e) *because* your net profit is so low.
f) *However*, if your expansion project succeeds,
g) He should *also* make some comments

Note the following, which do not introduce a logical relation but show the attitude of the writer:

Please instruct your Financial Controller. (requesting)
Fortunately this is not a serious problem at present. (pleased)

I Reading III

A question of costing

Extract from a memorandum from the Financial Controller giving details of a new costing system which he intends to instal:

Analysis
My department has examined the costing methods used to decide product selling prices and profitability and we have found several methodological errors, particularly in the allocation of overheads to products. We therefore recalculated the current unit costs of two major products (including the Protocap Energy Saver) using activity costing methods. This meant we costed them on the basis of activities such as production, buying, quality control, handling and storage and maintenance.

The result showed that the current method significantly overstates the cost of the Protocap and that the reported cost is lower and the selling price could be lowered.

Under the present costing system overheads are given as a percentage of labour expenditures, based on historical data. This method ensures that all overheads are absorbed or charged to products but does not calculate the corrected actual cost of resources used in the production of a product.

Proposed Solution
We should establish the cost of the contribution of each activity to each unit, and then charge products their share of all the contributing activities.

This will be done by calculating the forecast or budgeted cost of each major activity and determining which product factor drives or influences that activity. The cost driver may be expressed in various ways - in terms of hours, volume of actions, orders, inspection, etc.

The main categories of overhead expenditure or activities for which a cost driver rate will be established are:

Material procurement	Material handling and storage
Production set-up	Maintenance
Quality control	Machinery department
Fitting department	Packing and dispatch

Finance department staff will visit departmental managers to discuss which activities drive the costs which arise in each department.

Note: Vocabulary items not mentioned in the Vocabulary section below may have been dealt with in an earlier unit. Use the Index and Glossary to check.

J Vocabulary

1 Cost, cost, cost Intransitive verb
cost, costed, costed Transitive verb

The verb *to cost* has two past forms, depending how it is being used. Notice the differences between the formation of past and present perfect in the examples:

The whole trip *cost* her £340.
This holiday has *cost* me a small fortune.
They *costed* freight and marine insurance into the price.
The Financial Controller has *costed* elements of each activity and allocated them to the relevant products.

Dictionary work

Word families

2 Study and try to complete the table below.
Notice that, while there are some patterns, they are not reliable. For example if you know the adjective form of *analysis* as *analytical* you would expect the adjective of *synthesis* to be synthetical* but it is *synthetic*:

Noun	*Verb*	*Adjective*	*Adverb*
synthesis	synthesise	synthetic	synthetically
–..........	analyse	....	analytically
–..........	(use systematise)	methodical methodological	methodically methodologically
–..........	–	historical	....
–..........	....	contributory	–
significance	signify	significant	....
–..........	–	active	actively

3 Now complete these sentences with words from the table.

a) The new approach to costing makes a .... difference in the calculations of profitability of the Protocap.
b) Frequently it pays to re-think the .... used to cost business activity.
c) The Financial Controller decided to .... the system in use at Proteus Manara.
d) It will be necessary to set a value on the .... made by each activity to the cost of each product.
e) The .... cost of an asset is the amount that was paid for it when it was bought.
f) Production, quality control, packing and despatch are examples of .... on which costing can be based.

How synonymous are synonyms?

4 Decide which of the synonyms should be used with each phrase: (Line numbers for words in Reading III are shown in brackets.)

a) current (6) present (14)
a .... account; the .... government; several people were .... in the room; the .... rate of growth; the .... issue of the Accountancy Journal; "That's all for the ...., thank you."

b) examine (1) look at
We've .... the causes of the delays. He .... the figures in great detail. At the end of the course, he was .... thoroughly on the subject. This morning we're going to .... some aspects of costing.

c) decide (2) establish (20)
The methods used to .... the true cost are incorrect. They .... to change the system. The company was .... in 1864. The court .... the cause of death.

d) calculate (23) work out (recalculate (5) = work out again)
She .... the answer on paper. The engineer .... the size of the beams needed for the building. They .... a solution to the problem.

e) factor (24) influence (25)
The profit margin was reduced due to several .... The artist said there were several .... in his work.

f) category (28) class
They stayed in a top .... hotel. There are several .... of cost driver at Proteus. Arthur Ashe was a world .... tennis player. The activities mentioned by the accountant are different .... of overhead.

g) express (25) give (14)
The figure was .... as a percentage. He .... a large figure as the price he would pay. He .... his 'phone number. The first part was .... in letters.

5 Now go over each pair again and try to make rules for using each word.

6 Use the groups of related words to arrive at a word in the text.

a) locus, locate, location, locality .... *(paragraph 1)*
b) port, porter, re-exported, transported, ... *(paragraph 2)*
c) source of a river, resourceful .... *(paragraph 3)*
d) forward, before, cast-off, outcast, ... *(paragraph 5)*

7 Complete the following sentences using words from the previous exercise. Put the words in the right form.

a) The .... currency of Proteus financial statements is normally Manara dollars.
b) The newspaper .... a dividend of 3 pence per share.
c) The older employees were a useful .... of information for the new Financial Controller.
d) The accountant decided that the old method .... too many costs to each unit.

8 How are the following ideas expressed?

a) Mistakes in the way something is done *(2 words, paragraph 1)*
b) Assigning indirect costs *(3 words, paragraph 1)*
c) exaggerates *(1 word, paragraph 2)*
d) The cost mentioned in the last annual accounts *(2 words, paragraph 2)*
e) The new cost figure arrived at after revising the method of calculating it *(3 words, paragraph 3)*
f) labour, capital, land, machinery, raw materials *(1 word, paragraph 3)*
g) predicted *(1 word, paragraph 5)*
h) The cost planned in advance *(2 words, paragraph 5)*
i) The particular needs of a product which produces action in such areas as quality control and packaging and distribution *(2 words, paragraph 5)*

Activities

9 Look through Reading III and give some examples of activities.

Formal and informal

10 Match the formal accountancy expressions on the left with the less formal equivalents on the right.

Material procurement	Wrapping up
Production set-up	Keeping in working order
Quality control	Buying things
Fitting department	Putting things together
Material handling and storage	Sending things
Maintenance	Getting ready to make
Packing	Moving and keeping
Despatch	Checking

K Grammar reference

1 **Present perfect** (See Unit 2 N Grammar 6, p.28)

Examples

My department has examined the costing methods used to decide product selling prices (*line 1*)

and we have found several methodological errors (*line 3*)

2 **'... based in Birmingham ...'** (See Unit 1 F Grammar 1 & 2 p.8)

Examples

... the costing methods used to decide selling prices ... (*line 1*)

... based on historical data. (*line 15*)

... the corrected actual cost of resources used in the production of a product (*lines 17 - 18*)

3 **Purposive 'to'**

Finance department staff will visit departmental managers to discuss which activities drive the costs which arise in each department. (*lines 34 - 36*)

4 **Advising / recommending**

(Unit 3, D Grammar 1, p. 33)

Example

We should establish the cost of the contribution of each activity. (*line 20*)

L Grammar from Reading III

Sentence connectors

Phrases can be used at the beginnings of sentences to show a logical connection with previous sentences. Examples of logical connections are *reason, result, contrast* and *time sequence.*

Examples of connectors showing *result:*

We therefore recalculated the current unit costs of ... (*lines 5 - 6*)

This meant (that) we costed them (*line 8*)

The result showed (that) the current method ... (*lines 11 - 13*)

and that the reported cost is lower ...

and (that) the selling price could be lowered.

This method ensures that all overheads are absorbed ... (*line 16*)

1 Can you complete the pairs of sentences using illustrations from your own work situation or an industrial example in your country?

a) A fire burnt down the main factory. We therefore .... This meant that ....

b) A new .... system was introduced last year. The result showed (that) ....

c) They use a unique system in the factory. This method ensures (that) ....

Instrumental 'by'

2 Compare these two examples:
He sat up all night drinking cans of beer.
He got drunk by drinking too much beer.

The first example answers the question
'What did he do all night?'
The second example answers the question
'How did he get drunk?'

Now look at:

This will be done *by calculating* the forecast or budgeted cost of each major activity and *(by) determining* which product factor drives or influences that activity. (*lines 23 - 25*)

What question does the above sentence answer?

We therefore recalculated the current unit costs of two major products (including the Protocap Energy Saver) using activity costing methods.

What question does the above sentence answer?

3 Decide whether the following sentences should use *by* before the *– ing* form of the verb.

a) How did he revive the finances of the company?
He did it / sacking half the workers.
b) What did he do at the company?
He revived its finances / using some accountancy software.
c) What did they do after the fire?
They rebuilt the warehouse / taking several months to complete the job.
d) How did they rebuild the warehouse?
They did / recycling the old building materials.

M Discussion

Ask and answer the questions, working in pairs or small groups.

1 How did the methodological errors affect costing at Proteus?
2 What did the Financial Controller do at first?
3 What did he base his calculations on?
4 What did he discover about the reported cost of the Protocap?
5 How were overheads given under the previous system of calculating unit costs?
6 What was the basis of calculating the contribution of overheads?
7 Why was the old system of unit costing wrong?
8 What was the Financial Controller's proposed solution?
9 How could they decide what proportion of the activities in the company could be added to unit costs?

10 Can you give an example of an activity?
11 Can you give another?
12 Anything else?
13 What's that?
14 Can you explain that?
15 How will the finance department staff find out which activities drive the costs arising in each department?

N Listening

Dialogue 1

The Financial Controller is talking with his subordinate, the Financial Accountant. They are discussing changes which must be made to make the Proteus accounting system conform fully with group accounting procedures. They also have to ensure that the system produces the information needed to develop an improved cost accounting system based on activity costing.

1 Listen to the tape and complete the tapescript.

FC I see that .... has been running on the minicomputer for nine months. So you and your staff should be familiar with each ....

FA Yes, it was difficult at the beginning, and we had to use .... a lot and we did find a .... But on the whole we got good ....

FC Well I hope those bugs .... because now we've got to make some changes to the whole system.

FA Changes now? Isn't it rather late in the day for changes? Our .... ends in only four months.

FC I think it'll be OK. The software itself won't have to be modified. But we must make greater use of .... so as to produce the additional information which the Group Finance Department needs and to develop an .... Later next year, we shall probably .... another company on the system.

FA Will that be .... subsidiary or an associated company?

FC It could be either. In any case we must be ready to use the system to produce ....

Dialogue 2

The Financial Controller continues his conversation with the Financial Accountant. They go on to talk about things they will have to do as a result of making changes in the Proteus accounting system.

Listen to the tape and complete the tapescript:

FC In any case we must be ready to use the system to produce ....

FA That means we'll .... whole .... It'll affect ...., the Cost Centre Codes, even the Departmental codes.

FC That's certainly true. But don't forget we must still be able to produce our local Manaran .... in the .... laid down by the Accounting Law. So we can't change ....too much.

FA It shouldn't be a problem. The software allows us to use two sets of .... We could use one set for UK .... and the other for Manaran Statutory Accounts. We can also add .... to the Nominal Ledger code to allow us to ....

FC Excellent! Now let's see. For each activity we'll have to calculate .... as well as the revenue and expenses which it generates.

FA It's going to take a lot of work to calculate expenses by activity such as ...., ..., ..., the cost of space used, insurance and so on.

FC Yes, you're right there. The problem is to decide which activities we must use. We definitely need .... expenses in the areas of ...., materials handling, ..., production, ..., selling and after-sales service.

FA The list is endless. I'd better talk to the departmental managers and ....in their areas. Mind you, we could end up with too many activities.

O Game

Language aim: to practise using the vocabulary of this unit in complete sentences.

Procedure:

1 Write each of the sentences below on pieces of paper or card.
2 Cut each sentence in half where indicated.
3 Put all the first halves of sentences in one pile (Pile A).
4 Put all the second halves of sentences in another pile (Pile B).
5 Shuffle both piles.
6 Deal out all pile A round the group.
7 Deal out all pile B round the group.
8 Everyone should now go round all the other members of the group asking for pieces of sentences until they have completed their sentences. They may exchange half-sentences blind - this means without telling their exchange partner what it is they are offering.

The winner is the one who has the largest number of complete sentences first.

	A	B
a)	There are various costing methods which can be used to	decide product selling prices and profitability.
b)	The Financial Controller found several methodological errors, particularly in	the allocation of overheads to products.
c)	They recalculated the current unit costs of two major products	(including the Protocap Energy Saver) using activity costing methods.
d)	Products can be costed on the basis of activities such as	production, buying, quality control, handling and storage and maintenance.
e)	Some methods may significantly overstate the cost of the Protocap	so that the reported cost is lower and the selling price can be reduced.
f)	Under one costing system overheads may be given as a percentage of labour	expenditures, based on historical data.
g)	The old method ensures that all overheads are	absorbed or charged to products.
h)	But the old method does not calculate the corrected actual cost	of resources used in the production of a product.
i)	The new costing method establishes the cost of the contribution of each activity to each unit	and then charges products their share of all the contributing activities.
j)	The forecast or budgeted cost of each major activity is calculated and the product factor	which drives or influences that activity is determined.
k)	The cost driver may be expressed in various ways	– in terms of hours, volume of actions, orders, inspection etc.

l)	Two of the main categories of overhead expenditure or activities for which a cost driver rate	will be established are: material procurement and material handling and storage.
m)	Finance department staff may need to visit departmental managers	to discuss which activities drive the costs which arise in each department.
n)	They costed freight and	marine insurance into the price.
o)	The Financial Controller costed the elements of each	activity and allocated them to the relevant products.
p)	Frequently it pays to re-think the	methods used to cost business activity.
q)	It will be necessary to set a value on the contribution	made by each activity to the cost of each product.
r)	The historical cost of an asset is the amount that was	paid for it when it was bought.
s)	Production, quality control, packing and despatch are examples	of activities on which costing can be based.
t)	A directive from Head Office stated Group policy that	the Protocap was to become the flagship product of the Group and sales should be increased.
u)	Another memorandum from Head Office pointed out several weaknesses in	the Proteus Manara Balance Sheet and Profit and Loss account.
v)	Proteus Manara will not be able to reach its target return on capital from sales in the EC, due to	intense domestic competition and low margins.
w)	This leaves the development of	export markets as a possible way forward.
x)	The task force should carry out desk research to obtain	information on markets, business conditions and competitors.
y)	Before exporting to a country or even visiting it, Proteus	will carry out as much desk research as possible.

UNIT 6 Evaluating a Project

A Introduction

The story so far

The management of Proteus Manara have decided that the only way out of their problems is to expand into Central and Eastern Europe. Three weeks ago the Managing Director set up a task force to carry out desk research. The people concerned were the Financial Controller and the Production and Marketing Managers.

They reviewed accounting procedures, production methods and marketing prospects. One result, among others, was a complete revision of costing methods which meant that the chief product of Proteus - the Protocap Energy Saver - could in fact be sold at a lower price and still make a profit.

The Manara Managing Director hoped to satisfy the Group Chairman that he could solve problems of gross profit levels and financial structure. His other financial problem was how to raise capital for the proposed expansion project. So far, he was unable to go to an international market and had to rely on raising capital in Manara.

This unit is about:

a Business evaluations
b Assessing country risk
c Contingent liabilities
d Raising capital

He was unable to go to an international market and had to rely on raising capital in Manara.

B Reading I

Memorandum: Group guidelines for business evaluations

1 The Managing Director of Proteus (Manara) Ltd has the memorandum on file. Part of the memo is quoted below:

It explains the Group requirements for capital projects of all subsidiaries.

2 Extract from the memorandum

NOTE ON MAJOR INVESTMENT PROJECTS

Acquisitions of fixed capital or long-term assets worth £100,000 or more (or the equivalent in other currencies) count as major projects. Such major projects must take account of the need to make an adequate return and the risks inherent in the country where the investment is being made.

What is considered to be an adequate return will depend on the amount of political or economic risk involved in the project.

The Group Board emphasises the importance of maintaining effective control of all current investments and requires post-implementation audits to be carried out within six months of the completion of a project.

The above applies to all acquisitions, whether assets are bought for cash or with the help of long-term borrowing, or whether they are leased or rented. It also applies to construction projects as well as to the purchase of existing businesses. Additionally, it covers the formation of new companies through mergers or through joint ventures with third parties.

C Vocabulary

1 Find words in the text with the same meaning as the following expressions.

a) An asset which has been bought
b) Money received as a result of an investment
c) Creation or making
d) the joining together of companies
e) belonging to as part of

2 Now use the words to complete these sentences.

a) SmithKline Beecham was formed by the .... of Beecham of the UK and the US company Smith Kline & French.
b) The privatisation policies of the new governments in Central Europe led to the .... of many new companies.
c) Several Western companies came to the East looking for cheap ....
d) They realised that it would be some years before they would get an acceptable .... for their outlay.
e) There were a number of .... difficulties in the project.

Noun phrases

3 Use words from the box to re-make compound noun phrases from the passage and to complete the sentences. (The number of words in each noun phrase is indicated in brackets):

borrowing	ventures	audits	assets	current	long	
investments	term	existing	joint	third	post	fixed
long	parties	term	implementation	capital	businesses	

a) The chief shareholders insisted on full *(3 words)*.................... before agreeing to allow their money to be used for the new company.
b) The agreement signed by the two companies allowed for a *(2 words)*.................... to purchase shares in the venture.
c) Because of the economic recession, there was a surplus of factory premises and similar *(3 words)*.................... on the market.
d) The Eurobond market is used by multinationals and governments to finance the purchase of *(3 words)*.................... which are paid off within ten years.
e) There were so many projects in progress that the Managing Director decided to review all *(2 words)*.................... .
f) Such a large project could only be financed by *(3 words)*.................... .
g) In many ways it is easier for *(2 words)*.................... than a start-up company to borrow money because they have a track record to show the bank when asking for a loan.
h) A very large number of *(2 words)*.................... of Western and Eastern partners have been set up since 1989.

Adjectives

4 Replace the adjectives with more formal equivalents from the reading passage.

a) big
b) enough
c) present
d) useful
e) ongoing

Use of verbs

5 Use the verbs from the box in an appropriate form, and in the same sense as they are used in the passage, to complete the sentences.

count as	maintain	carry out	apply	lease	rent

a) The business .... the office for ten years.
b) International Accounting Standards .... to the interpretation of contingent liabilities.
c) They decided .... premises until there was an opportunity to buy a more suitable building.
d) For the purposes of this account unfinished goods .... work in progress.
e) The work was .... immediately.
f) The quality control manager's job is to ....the standards of craftsmanship in the workshop.

D Grammar

Understood words

Sometimes words are omitted because they are understood through the context:

Example
the equivalent = the equivalent sum / amount / figure
(= *an amount equal in value*)

1 Identify the 'understood words' at the * sign in the following sentences.

a) Here's part of the money I owe you. I'll give you the rest * later.
b) He wanted to know why the bank had charged him. When he went there, they explained why *.
c) He liked the book so much that he went to the library and got out another * by the same author.
d) She paid half the invoice in cash and the balance * by cheque.

Prepositions

2 Complete the sentences with the best choice of preposition.

a) They accepted shares / *value* / *worth* / *amount* / *cost* / £10,000 as security for the loan.
b) He asked the foreign exchange clerk what £300 was / *by* / *in* / *with* / *as* / Swiss francs.
c) Assessment of risk depends / *to* / *with* / *of* / *on* / the sort of country you are dealing with.
d) Several banks were involved / *in* / *with* / *by* / *over* / the fraud.
e) In the / *after* / *post* / *before* / *successive* / revolution period, many countries faced considerable hardships.

f) The audit was carried / *over* / *on* / *out* / *off* / in July.
g) The project will be completed / *within* / *inside* / *before* / six months.
h) The rule applies / *to* / *for* / *with* / *in* / all companies in EC countries.
i) They sold the car / *with* / *for* / *in* / *at* / cash.
j) The project went ahead / *with* / *by* / *through* / the help of a bank loan.
k) Several new companies were formed / *with* / *through* / *under* / *by* / joint ventures / *by* / *with* / *from* / *of* / third parties.

E Discussion

1 Read the questions below and make sure that you can answer them.

2 Then, working with a partner, ask and answer the questions without looking back at the reading passage.

What counts as a major project for Proteus?
What must such projects take account of?
What types of risk does a company take with overseas investments?
What should a Proteus subsidiary do about current investments?
What else should it do?
What sort of acquisitions could Proteus (Manara) make?
What other sorts could it make?
Anything else?
How many different forms of foreign investment were mentioned?

F Reading II and Activity

Country risk

The scale on the next page was devised by Business Environment Risk Information of the College of Business and Economics, University of Delaware, USA. It lists a number of factors which you should take into account when assessing the risk of investing in a country.

1 Before attempting the assessment, read the scale and discuss the vocabulary with your trainer.

2 To obtain a result, choose any country and assign a number of points to it for each factor. The range is from 0.0 (= not acceptable) to 4.0 (= extraordinarily favourable).

Index for Analysis of Country Risks

		Number of points	X Weighting	Total rating
1	Political stability		X 3.0	
2	Attitude towards foreign investor and profit		X 1.5	
3	Nationalisation		X 1.5	
4	Monetary inflation		X 1.5	
5	Economic growth		X 2.5	
6	Labour cost/productivity		X 2.0	
7	Balance of payments		X 1.5	
8	Current convertibility		X 2.5	
9	Bureaucratic delays		X 1.0	
10	Enforceability of contracts		X 1.5	
11	Professional services and contractors		X 0.5	
12	Local management of partners		X 1.0	
13	Communication and transport		X 1.0	
14	Short-term credit (availability on local market)		X 2.0	
15	Long-term loans and venture capital (availability on local market)		X 2.0	
Total				

(See the Answer Key for an evaluation of your score.)

G Reading III

Accounting treatment of contingent liabilities

The crucial question facing the Proteus Manara Board is how to finance their proposed expansion. They would need to persuade their bank to lend money, or the parent company in Birmingham to increase their investment. Whoever provides the money, whether it is the bank (in Manara) acting as lender, or the Group (in Birmingham) acting as investor, will want to have a clear and true picture of Proteus's financial health as shown by the latest Balance Sheet.

How a company's liabilities are treated in the Balance Sheet can have a strong influence on potential investors. On the other hand contingent liabilities are not shown in the Balance Sheet but must by law be disclosed in a note in the annual accounts. They are losses or expenses which might or might not happen depending on whether certain events occur. Any investor or lender considering putting money into Proteus's project, will therefore want to read the annual accounts, as well as the Balance Sheet, in full.

Here is an example of disclosure of contingent liabilities in the statutory accounts of Proteus Limited:

	1994 £m	1995 £m
Proteus Ltd		
Borrowings guaranteed	8	6
Other contingent liabilities	23	19
Other subsidiaries		
Other contingent liabilities	12	14

Unquantified claims have been made against the Group undertakings relating to product liability and intellectual property rights. In the opinion of the Directors the amounts provided in the accounts against such claims are adequate.

H Vocabulary

Using adjectives

1 Find *one* adjective from the paragraph indicated which can be used with all the nouns in each group.

Example
Importance, significance – *crucial*

a) Importance, significance (*paragraph 1*)
b) project, plan, scheme (*paragraph 1*)
c) organisation, company (*paragraph 1*)
d) view, plan, idea (*paragraph 1*)
e) picture, story, account of the facts (*paragraph 1*)
f) sales, markets, business, customers (*paragraph 2*)

g) currency, wind, leader, man (*paragraph 2*)
h) report, general meeting, payment, subscription, (*paragraph 2*)
i) development, cost (*paragraph 4*)
j) funds, space, accommodation, food (*paragraph 4*)

2 Find an adjective from the paragraphs indicated which can be used to complete the sentences.

a) The question of finance was .... to the success of the project. (*paragraph 1*)
b) When investing in another country one needs to have a .... idea of the risks involved. (*paragraph 1*)
c) The .... *Times* is an easily recognisable newspaper because it is printed on pink paper. (*paragraph 1*)
d) Have you heard the .... news? (*paragraph 1*)
e) .... politicians have made political capital out of expressing racist views. (*paragraph 2*)
f) New .... rules have been made for private companies. (*paragraph 3*)

Special terms

3 Find the following expressions in the reading passage:

contingent liabilities
disclosure
statutory accounts
borrowings guaranteed
unquantified claims
product liability
intellectual property rights
annual accounts

Now complete these sentences using appropriate expressions from the list.

a) All public companies are obliged by law to publish .... each year.
b) They have to follow rules of .... in the way their accounts are presented.
c) .... concern the ownership of new scientific and technical ideas as well as inventions and publications.
d) .... are ones which cannot be assessed.
e) Companies have to take out ....insurance in case one of their products causes an accident.
f) .... are possible expenses which may have to be paid at any time.
g) All possible loss which depends on certain events happening, must be included in the ....
h) They promised to repay a bank loan granted to their subsidiary company in case the subsidiary failed to repay it. The amount of the loan was then given as a note to their annual accounts under contingent liabilities as ....

Useful verbs

4 Use verbs from the paragraphs indicated to complete the sentences.

a) Financial problems must be .... at an early stage of any expansion project. (*paragraph 1*)
b) The directors considered how to .... the expansion. (*paragraph 1*)
c) They would have to .... a backer to invest in the company. (*paragraph 1*)
d) Another possibility was for the existing shareholders to .... their investment. (*paragraph 1*)
e) Perhaps the bank would .... a loan. (*paragraph 1*)
f) Liabilities may be .... in different ways in the accounts. (*paragraph 2*)
g) Professional consultants should never .... business affairs of their clients to others. (*paragraph 2*)
h) The accident .... early this morning. (*paragraph 2*)
i) Accidents .... frequently at that crossing. (*paragraph 2*)
j) The Manara board .... how best to finance the project. (*paragraph 2*)
k) Sometimes the amount of claims which .... against a company are not known at the time of publication of the Balance Sheet. (*paragraph 4*)

Lexical cohesion devices

English speakers are not happy with repetition and use various means of avoiding it. One of these is the use of an equivalent phrase, which is also used to make the text hang together, or give it 'cohesion'. Instead of repeating the phrase, something giving the same force or meaning, or an 'equivalent' is used. In this way 'non-technical' expressions carry a technical value.

5 Say what the following examples refer to:

a) *lend money* (*line 2*) refers to one word in line 1.
b) *provides* (*line 4*) refers to one word in line 2.
c) *potential investors* (*line 9*) refers to two words in lines 4 and 5.
d) *losses or expenses* (*line 11*) refers to two words in lines 9 - 10.

They needed to persuade their bank to ...

1 Use the notes to make sentences like the example:

They (persuade) .. .... bank .. lend .... money.
They persuaded their bank to lend them money.

a) Competition at home (force) .... them .... look for export markets.
b) The law (require) .... public limited companies .... show contingent liabilities in the annual accounts. (*Use the present tense.*)
c) The Managing Director (urge) .... the task force .... find a solution.
d) They (compel) .... ask the bank for a loan. (*Use the passive.*)

... as shown by ...

They need a clear and true picture .. (show) .. the Balance Sheet.
They need a clear and true picture as shown by the Balance Sheet.

2 Complete the sentences in the same way:

a) They introduced a new costing system (explain).................... the Financial Controller.
b) The new system (demonstrate).................... the Accounts Manager would put the Protocap Energy Saver into profit.
c) The bank accepted the accounts (prepare).................... the accountant.
d) The new law (announce).................... the government yesterday comes into effect at midnight.

Grammatical cohesion devices: reference words

In order to make a text cohere without repetition, grammatical forms such as pronouns and determiners are used which refer back to ideas already mentioned.

3 Which words do the following refer to?

a) They (*line 2*)
b) their (*line 3*)
c) They (*line 11*)
d) the Group (*line 24*)
e) such claims (*line 26*)

J Discussion

1 Ask and answer questions about Reading III.

What crucial question faces the Proteus Manara board?
What are the two possibilities for financing their proposed expansion?
What will the provider of the money want to have?
What will potential investors want to see apart from the Balance Sheet?

What can have a strong influence on potential investors?
What are contingent liabilities?
Are contingent liabilities shown in the balance sheet?
Where are contingent liabilities disclosed?
How can contingent liabilities be seen by potential investors?
What examples of contingent liabilities are mentioned in the passage?

2 Continue making your own questions in the same way and putting them to your colleagues.

K Listening I

Suggesting possibility

A potential liability

The Financial Controller (FCM) of Proteus Manara is on the phone to the Manager of the Treasury Department (MTD) of the parent company in Birmingham.

1 Look at the following explanations of words and phrases used in the conversation:

a) *Local currency borrowings* (Manara dollars)
b) It *soared* like a rocket.
c) *Collateral* is something given to the bank against a loan.
d) A *parent company guarantee* is a promise.
e) *Realise*: to produce money by a sale.
f) *Customised* trucks are designed for a customer.
g) *Reluctant to give guarantees*: they don't want to promise anything.
h) *Subject to fluctuations*: it tends to go up and down.
i) *Letter of Comfort* (see Glossary)
j) *Accounting Standard*: rules for all accountants
k) *UK statutory accounts*: the law says companies must keep correct accounts.

2 Now read the gapped dialogue below. Listen to the conversation on the cassette, which introduces some new accounting expressions and practises more modals and other ways of expressing possibility or impossibility. Then listen a second time and complete the tapescript:

FCM Look, I really need to discuss our .... As you must have read from my report, we're having a difficult time this year and our borrowings have soared.

MTD Yes, that was quite a jump, wasn't it!

FCM The latest problem is that our bankers here .... any more money on the strength of our 1994 financial statements. They want security. They're asking for either .... or a ....

MTD Well, what collateral have you got?

FCM Unfortunately, since we rent our factory, we .... machinery and vehicles. I suspect .... the vehicles. Our machinery is too specialised and .... much on a .... And the vehicles are mainly customised trucks.

MTD Well, as you know, the Group Directors are reluctant to give guarantees, especially to overseas operations and the more so where the potential liability is in a currency .... Do you think .... a Letter ....?

FCM No, I've already asked them. They prefer a guarantee in Manara dollars.

MTD Well, at present the Group policy is to keep .... to a minimum, ever since the Accounting Standard has required them to be reported in the UK ....

L Listening II

1 The Financial Controller of Proteus (Manara) continues his phone conversation with the Manager of the Treasury Department of the parent company.

2 Study the vocabulary explanations:

a) A concrete proposal: suggestion based on hard fact
b) Cross guarantee: one not from the parent but a sister company
c) Sterling: UK currency
d) Eurodollar: expatriate American currency
e) Approves: thinks well of
f) The deadline: After this, it is too late

3 Read the gapped dialogue below. Listen to the tape. Then listen again and complete the tapescript. (Some spaces have more than one word.)

FCM Well, I must get back to our bankers with a concrete proposal within the next ten days. What do you suggest?

MTD I'll talk to the Group Financial Director. Logically we have .... – one is a parent company guarantee or a .... from another European subsidiary with assets free, as collateral – and that's complicated enough! Failing that, we .... either a direct sterling or Eurodollar loan. Lastly we .... a direct investment in Proteus Manara.

FCM Obviously, the last would be preferable, especially since we are planning this major expansion in Central and Eastern Europe.

MTD I agree. But that depends on whether the Main Board approves your expansion project. Look, we ought to try to persuade your bankers not to insist on a guarantee, at least until a decision is reached on the Manara project.

FCM Yes, I agree entirely. It does occur to me that, if the Group Financial Director .... to Manara and have a meeting with our bankers, he .... them that Birmingham .... you. .... he not invite them to Birmingham, to see the main Proteus factory? Then they .... a Letter of Comfort or postpone the deadline for a guarantee.

MTD It's certainly worth a try. Let me talk to the chief and I'll fax you an answer within 48 hours.

M Grammar

Suggesting possibility

1 Look at how *could* and *might* are used in the dialogues to suggest possibility:

a) ... we could only offer machinery and vehicles.
b) ... we could either make a direct sterling or Eurodollar loan
c) Lastly we could make a direct investment in Proteus Manara.
d) ... he might convince them that Birmingham might support you.
e) Or could he not invite them to Birmingham, to see the main Proteus factory?
f) Then they might accept a Letter of Comfort or postpone the deadline for a guarantee.

The difference? In practice, very little. Both are used to suggest possibilty, though *might* is perhaps more tentative:-

- We *could go* for a drink after supper.
- He might lend you money if you ask him nicely.

N Game

1 Write the following words on slips of paper.

2 Deal them out to the group.

3 The first to make a reasonable sentence is the winner.

Acquisitions	The Group Board	The note on projects
fixed capital assets	effective control	the formation of new companies
major projects	post-implementation audits	through mergers
	within six months of completion	through joint ventures

UNIT 7 Reviewing the Financial Base

A Introduction

The story so far

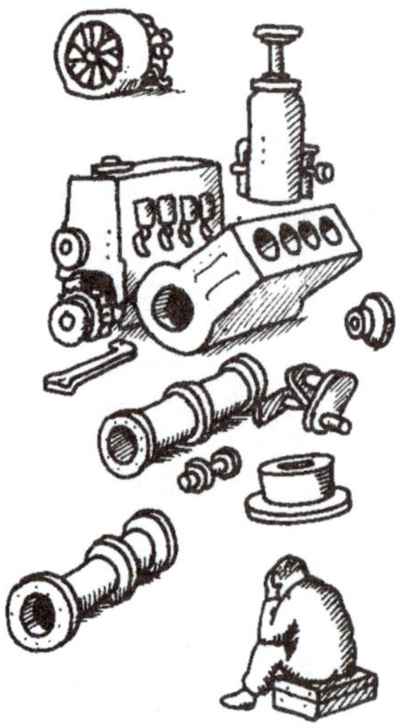

Proteus (Manara) Ltd, the electrical subsidiary of the Proteus Group in Birmingham, have decided to expand into Central Europe and have been supported in principle by the Group Main Board. Earlier, they had problems of falling profits despite the increased sales of their flagship product, the Protocap Electrical Energy Saver.

The Proteus management in Manara reviewed the International Accounting Standard relating to contingent liabilities and discussed ways of raising capital for their expansion project. The three possibilities were to borrow from the bank; to ask the Group in Birmingham to increase their investment; or borrow on one of the international money markets.

Birmingham was reluctant to co-operate because of uncertainties over the value of the Manara Dollar and the need to disclose any contingent liability. In addition there was no taxation treaty between Britain and Manara, so profits of subsidiaries were liable to be taxed twice (See Unit 5 Reading II, p.62.)

Regarding management of the project, the management at Manara City decided that it would be best to find an existing company in the East to act as partner in a joint venture. The advantages of working with people who understood the local market and conditions of business were overwhelming. This left the overriding problem of funding.

This unit is about:

a The Proteus Annual Report and Accounts
b Press coverage of the Proteus Annual Report
c The Auditor's Report

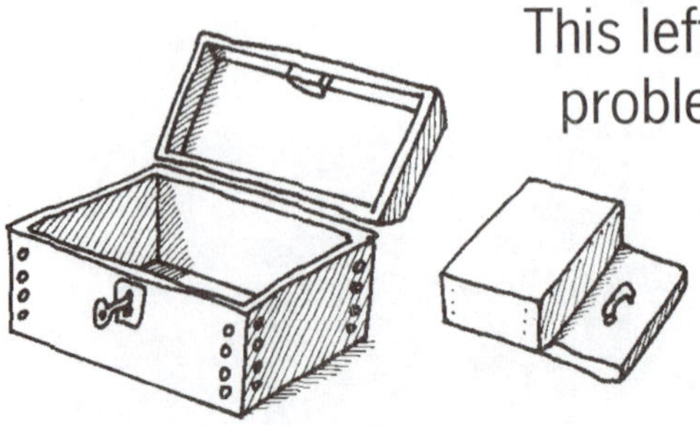

This left the overriding problem of funding...

B Reading I

The Annual Report

1 Introduction

Each year the Proteus Group publishes its Annual Report and Accounts for the financial year. The report begins with a statement to the shareholders by the chairperson. In it he or she reviews the results of the past year and forecasts what will happen in the coming year. (Note that a company in Britain can start its financial year in any month and so auditing work is spread evenly throughout the year.)

Next comes the Board of Directors' Report which is required by law. This gives an account of the activities of each director, of the Group, of the Group's employment policy and of money given to political parties and charities.

The Annual Accounts report to shareholders on the financial results of the Group's operations during the past year and show the financial position at the end of the year. The accounts are followed by the Auditor's Report and include the following reports:

- Consolidated Profit and Loss Account
- Consolidated Balance Sheet
- Cash flow statement
- Statement of Accounting Policies
- Notes to the Accounts

The document also includes a summary of the financial results for the past five years and gives general information about the company's share capital and the timetable for shareholders' meetings and the payment of dividends.

2 Extract from the Chairman's statement

> I am pleased to report a satisfactory performance of your company in the year just ended. Profit before tax increased by 18 per cent to £425 million and earnings per share increased by 15 per cent to 3.5 pence. Your Board has announced dividends for the year amounting in total to 10.5p per share, an increase of 13.5 per cent on the previous year. The growth in profits reflects the continuing progress in rationalising the business, more stable trading conditions at home and substantial advances in our programme for diversification.
>
> In our major export markets, we face fierce competition which depresses our earnings and threatens the profitability of our major new product - the Protocap Energy Saver. Your Board is actively seeking fresh overseas markets to consolidate Proteus's position as a major international supplier.

C Vocabulary

Terms explained in the text

1 Find the terms referred to:

a) A review of the results of the past year and a forecast of what will happen in the coming year *(8 words, paragraph 1)*
b) The period of time covered by the annual report *(2 words, paragraph 1)*
c) A collection of reports about the progress of the company over one year and forecast of its future *(4 words, paragraph 1)*
d) An account of the activities of the directors of the company, of employment policy and of money given for political and charitable purposes *(4 words, paragraph 2)*
e) A report to shareholders on the financial results of the group's operations during the past year, showing the financial position at the end of the year *(2 words, paragraph 3)*
f) A collection of statements including the Consolidated Profit and Loss Account, the Consolidated Balance Sheet, the Cash Flow Statement, a statement of accounting policies and a summary of the financial results for the past five years, some information about the company's share capital, the timetable for shareholders' meetings and the payment of dividends *(2 words, paragraph 3)*

Terms not explained in the text

2 Look up the following expressions in the Glossary:

employment policy
Consolidated Profit and Loss Account
Consolidated Balance Sheet
Cash Flow Statement
Statement of Accounting Policies
share capital
shareholders' meetings
earnings per share
dividends
rationalising
diversification
earnings

3 After looking up the expressions, take turns to ask other members of your group to explain each term, without looking at dictionaries, glossaries or notes. Begin with 'Can you explain..........?'

Using verbs

4 Choose the best verb from the box to complete each sentence.

require	include	report	announce	amount to	reflect	face
publish	depress	threaten	review	spread	seek	forecast

a) Each year public companies .... their Annual Reports and Accounts.
b) The report .... the results of the past year.
c) It also .... what is going to happen in the following year.
d) It is helpful to .... the work evenly throughout the year.
e) These reports and financial statements .... by law.
f) The report .... a summary of the financial results over the previous five years.
g) The Chairman .... on the performance of the company.
h) The board of directors .... a large dividend.
i) The dividend .... 10.5 pence per share.
j) The growth in profits .... the progress of the company.
k) They .... strong competition in overseas markets.
l) The competition .... earnings and
m) .... the profitability of the product in overseas markets.
n) The board of directors .... fresh overseas markets to counter the effect of competition.

5 Note the use of the verb *increase* in the examples:

A Profit before tax increased by 18 per cent to £425 million.
B Earnings per share increased by 15 per cent to 10.5 pence.

See Unit 2, E3.

Adjectives

6 Which adjective from the selection below can be used with all the nouns in each group?

fierce	major	fresh	political	consolidated	general	financial
satisfactory	the previous	annual	stable	substantial	export	the coming

a) loan, freight, Balance Sheet, Profit and Loss Account, position
b) forecast, problems, report, documents, information
c) information, advantages, purpose
d) decision, situation, party, developments
e) development, fruit, vegetables, food
f) product, development, decision, company, importance
g) arguments, competition, opposition, battles
h) report, meeting, review, event, conference
i) year, meeting, term, month, week
j) year, meeting, competition, term, month, week
k) results, figures, outcome, performance, position
l) conditions, situation, relationship, marriage
m) sum of money, amounts, sums, profits, losses

D Grammar

Use of the present simple in explanation

Examples:

A Each year the Proteus Group publishes its Annual Report.

B The report begins with a statement to the shareholders.

1 Go through the text and find ten more examples of this use of the verb.

Use of the passive

Examples

A Auditing work is spread evenly throughout the year.

B The Board of Directors' report is required by law

C This gives an account of money given to political parties.

D The accounts are followed by the Auditor's Report.

2 Use the notes to make similar sentences.

a) The annual report (publish) last week.

b) The Balance Sheet has a statement of money (spend) on research.

c) Expensive cars (give) to the directors' families.

d) Earnings (depress) by foreign competition.

e) Progress of the company (reflect) in the growth of profits.

E Discussion

Find one word for each numbered gap, without looking back at Reading I.

1 Introduction

Each year the Proteus Group publishes its Annual Report and (1) .... for the financial year. The report begins with a statement to the (2) .... by the chairperson. In it he or she reviews the results of the past year and (3) .... what will happen in the (4) .... year. (Note that a company in Britain can start its financial year in any month and so (5) .... work is spread evenly throughout the year.)

Next comes the Board of Directors' report which is (6) .... by law. This gives an account of the (7) .... of each director, of the group, of the group's employment policy and of (8) .... given to political parties and charities.

The (9) .... Accounts report to shareholders on the financial results of the group's (10) .... during the past year and show the financial (11) .... at the end of the year. The accounts are followed by the (12) .... Report and include the following reports:

Consolidated Profit and Loss Account
Consolidated Balance Sheet
Cash flow statement
Statement of Accounting Policies
Notes to the Accounts

The document also includes a (13) .... of the financial results for the past (14) .... years and gives general information about the company's (15).......... capital and the timetable for shareholders' (16) .... and the payment of (17) ....

2 Extract from the Chairman's statement

I am pleased to report a satisfactory (18).......... of your company in the year just ended. (19).......... before tax increased by 18 per cent to £425 million and (20).......... per share increased by 15 per cent to 3.5 pence. Your Board has (21).......... dividends for the year amounting in total to 10.5p per share, an increase of 13.5 per cent on the (22).......... year. The growth in profits (23).......... the continuing progress in rationalising the business, more (24).......... trading conditions at home and substantial (25).......... in our programme for diversification.

In our major export (26).........., we face fierce competition which depresses our (27).......... and threatens the profitability of our (28).......... new product - the Protocap Energy Saver. Your (29).......... is actively seeking fresh overseas markets to (30).......... Proteus's position as a major international supplier.

F Reading II

A newspaper report on the Proteus Group's published results

Before you read, think about the following:

a) Reports in the financial press, like the one below, summarise company results as they come out, all through the year.
b) If you were a shareholder of Proteus or an investor wondering whether to buy Proteus shares, what would you want to know from the newspaper article?
c) How will you assess the health of the company?

Despite the optimistic tone of the Chairman's Statement, the Proteus Group faces a difficult future. Its flagship product is already encountering strong price competition both at home and abroad.

The higher earnings per share obscures a deterioration in the Group's cash position, with borrowings up by 30 per cent. The Notes to the Accounts show that borrowings outside the UK now represent 40 per cent of total borrowings (against 28 per cent in the previous year). This means exposure to fluctuations in foreign interest rates and exchange rates. Also sterling's recent rise against most major currencies will result in lower reported global earnings and overseas net assets.

The Chairman admitted that expansion into Europe was an option being considered, possibly through a subsidiary, but was unwilling to go into detail. It is well known, however, that the Proteus company in Manara, where the Protocap is produced, is the most likely vehicle for further outward investment. The big question worrying the board and management at Manara is finance.

While the Group will rely heavily on its Energy Saver product range to boost sales, clearly it will not be possible to self-finance expansion solely from earnings. Also, in the present economic climate, shareholders may be reluctant to contribute for the second time in four years unless the Group can deliver higher dividends. Consequently the board is expected to finance the expansion almost entirely by borrowing and the gearing is expected to rise significantly. Analysts reacted cautiously to the Group's results by revising their profit forecast downwards. The share price fell slightly, leaving the P/E ratio at five times earnings.

G Vocabulary

1 Look up *product range*, *gearing* and *P/E ratio* in the Glossary.

2 How are the following ideas expressed in the passage?

a) The feeling that the future is going to be good (*2 words, paragraph 1*)
b) The company's increased income hides a reduction in its bank balance (*13 words, paragraph 2*)
c) Where foreign contingent liabilities are referred to (See Unit 6, p.81) (*4 words, paragraph 2*)
d) The company may lose money because of falls in the value of the Manara dollar. (*7 words, paragraph 2*)
e) Agreed when questioned that it was true. (*1 word, paragraph 3*)
f) Investing abroad was possible. (*8 words, paragraph 3*)
g) Method of putting money into a foreign venture (*5 words, paragraph 3*)
h) Pay for investment from the proceeds of sales (*6 words, paragraph 4*)
i) Unwilling to invest (*3 words, paragraph 4*)
j) So the company will fund the investment by bank loans. (*8 words, paragraph 4*)
k) The proportion of borrowings to shareholders' capital (*1 word, paragraph 4*)
l) They lowered their expectation that the company would do well. (*5 words, paragraph 4*).

Relationships of meaning

3 Note how the text is woven together by different relationships of meaning:

Examples from paragraph 1:

		Relationship
optimistic tone	facing a difficult future both at home and abroad	OPPOSITE
facing a difficult future	already encountering strong price competition	EQUIVALENT
facing	encountering	SYNONYM

Awareness of these relationships helps you to understand what you read.

4 Find the opposites of the expressions in italics.

a) The *higher earnings* per share (*6 words*)
b) sterling's recent *rise* (*1 word*)
c) The chairman *admitted* (*3 words*)
d) the group *will rely* (*5 words*)
e) *contribute* (*3 words*)
f) the board is expected *to finance* (*2 words*)
g) *optimistic* tone (*2 words*)

5 Find meanings equivalent to the following expressions

a) deterioration in the Group's cash position (*6 words*)
b) expansion ...possibly through a subsidiary (*7 words*)
c) a subsidiary (*5 words*)
d) expansion into Europe (*2 words*)
e) (boost) sales (*1 word*)

6 Finally, find a synonym for the following:

foreign interest rates (*1 word*)

Catchphrases used by financial journalists

7 Study the following expressions. Look carefully at how they are used in Reading II.

fluctuations in exchange rates
It is well known, however
obscure a deterioration in
by revising their forecast downwards
the optimistic tone of
Analysts reacted cautiously
fluctuations in interest rates
faces a difficult future
was an option being considered
are already encountering strong price competition
was unwilling to go into detail
in the present economic climate

8 Now use the expressions appropriately to complete the following report of a speech by the Prime Minister of Barakonia.

Despite .... Prime Minister's statement in the National Assembly last night, the country .... Its major products .... both at home and abroad.

The high wages and salaries .... in the country's balance of payments, with imports up by 30 per cent. Meanwhile the country is exposed to ....

Also the Barakonia Dinar's recent devaluation against most major currencies will result in lower income from exports and higher cost of imports.

The Prime Minister admitted that raising interest rates ...., possibly before the end of the month, but.......... .

.... that the Finance Minister, who is largely responsible for monetary policy, is the most likely supporter of higher interest rates. The big question worrying the government and ministry officials at Zamina .... is how the people of Barakonia will react to increased taxation.

.... to the Prime Minister's statement by .... of economic recovery ....

Useful adjectives

9 Which adjective from the box can be used in front of each group of nouns?

optimistic	difficult	price	total	the previous	foreign	exchange
recent	product	present	economic			

a) change, improvement, outlook, forecast, problems, system
b) control, rate, risk
c) future, problems, market, language, subject, negotiations
d) year, week, month, manager, government, prime minister, owner
e) country, language, food, travel, postage stamps, exchange
f) forecast, person, speech, statement
g) rise, control, change, increases, reduction
h) government, system, management, minister, difficulties, report
i) cost, failure, collapse, victory, success, saving
j) improvements, changes, developments, events, speech
k) improvements, changes, development, manager, research

Useful verbs

10 Choose the best verb from the box to complete each of the sentences.

face	show	represent	mean	result	consider	go into	worry
rely on	contribute	deliver	finance				

a) The project will be .... with the help of the National Bank of Manara.
b) The figures in the balance sheet .... large outstanding loans.
c) I didn't understand his remark. 'What do you ....?', I asked.
d) They .... every aspect of the problem.
e) We .... great detail over the case.
f) There's no need to ....about finding a partner yet.
g) You can .... him to arrive on time.
h) She .... several important points to the discussion.
i) We must .... the facts, even though they are unpleasant.
j) The plan .... a big improvement in the prospects of the company.
k) The changes in the costing system .... in improved profitability.
l) The Chinese restaurant will .... meals to your home.

Understanding technical terms

11 Are the following statements true or false?

a) The cash position of a company is the amount of cash it has in the bank.
b) The Notes to the Accounts have in them a note of contingent liabilities. (See Unit 6)
c) The word 'reported' means 'reported in the accounts'.
d) Outward investment means investment in another country.
e) Self-finance is paying for expansion out of capital accumulated from income.
f) Gearing is the proportion of loan capital to share capital in a company.
g) A flagship product is one in which a company is prepared to invest heavily to ensure its success.

12 Choose the best answer to complete each of these sentences.

a) *Results* as used in the last paragraph means
i) The annual accounts
ii) The Chairman's report
iii) The announced distribution of dividends
iv) The solution to Proteus's problem of finance

b) *Exposure* as used in the passage refers to
i) An exhibition of products
ii) Publication of the annual report and accounts
iii) A publicity campaign
iv) Risk

c) *Product range* is
i) the extent of the distribution of a product
ii) the life of a product
iii) a series of products related to each other
iv) a list of all the products made by one company

d) *P/E ratio* stands for
i) price/earnings ratio
ii) profit/earnings ratio
iii) performance/equity ratio
iv) premium/exemption ratio

H Grammar

The present continuous tense with 'already'

This use of the present continuous shows that something which was predictable is coming true.

Example:
Its flagship product is already encountering strong price competition both at home and abroad. (*lines 2-3*)

1 Make more examples of your own, using the notes.

a) Spring has come at last. ....flowers ....(open).
b) The snow has gone from the mountains. The rivers ....(flood).
c) It's 4 o'clock. The birds ....(sing).
d) The plans for the hospital are complete. They ....(dig) the foundations.
e) We reduced the price in August. Sales ....(rise).

Indirect speech or thought about current events

2 Note that the tenses of the verbs in each part of the sentence are the same.

Examples:
A The chairman *admitted* that expansion into Europe *was* an option being considered, ... (*line 11*)
B It *is* well-known, however, that the Proteus company in Manara *is* the most likely vehicle for further outward investment. (*lines 13 - 15*)

See Unit 2, N4, p.27 for more examples.

While

This use of 'while' shows concession:

Examples:
A While the Protocap is an excellent product, it will take some time for it to be established in the market.
B While the group will rely ... on its Energy Saver ... it will not be possible to self-finance expansion. (*lines 17 - 18*)

For shorter sentences it is more usual to use 'although':

C Although the city is beautiful, I prefer to live in the country.

3 Make your own examples from the notes, using *While*:
a) .... there are several advantages of using the Electrocut, the Protocap (be) better for our needs.
b) .... the idea of separation into separate states seemed to be the solution to all their problems, in fact the situation (be) worse for them after the split.
c) .... their governments set up an excellent health service and other social services, their industrial policies (lead to) pollution and other health problems.

Unless (present + future)

'Unless' is a more elegant way of saying 'if not':

Examples
A Shareholders won't put extra money into the company if it does not perform well. (future + *if* + *do/does* (*not*) + verb)
B Shareholders won't put extra money into the company, unless it performs well. (future + *unless* + present)

Other modals may be used besides *will* (e.g. *could, may, might, can*).

C Also, shareholders may be reluctant to contribute for a second time .... unless the group can deliver higher dividends. (present (*may*) + *unless* + *can* + verb) (*lines 19 - 21*)

You can also put *unless* at the beginning if you want to emphasise it:

D Unless you pay the money immediately, you won't get the goods.

4 Now make your own examples from the notes below.

a) .... difficult to do business in that country .... find a partner.
b) .... it rains soon, the plants .... die.
c) Many people .... die .... help (arrive) soon.
d) .... you service your car regularly, it .... (break down).
e) The shop .... take the video back .... (have) the receipt.
f) .... we go early, we .... get a seat in the restaurant.

I Listening

Explaining and comparing

Listen for the phrases used to explain the audit situation of the Manaran subsidiary of Proteus and comparing it with UK auditing practice. Then complete the tapescript. (Some spaces have more than one word.)

Auditor — I've brought an English translation of my Audit Report. The official version is in Manaran and has to be submitted to the Ministry of Finance at Manara City within the next ten days. But before submitting it, I want to .... with both of you.

MD — Thank you. But .... this report is of any use to our Head Office in Birmingham.

Auditor — As soon as I was appointed, I met the Financial Controller and .... for a Manaran audit. We both agreed that our auditing requirements ....the UK and I believe he passed on the information to your Head Office.

FC — Yes, I did. .... requirements are .... the UK auditing standards but ...., which means that a second audit usually .... by Manaran auditors appointed directly by Proteus.

MD (to FC) — So we have to pay for two audits!

FC — The Manaran audit is cheaper .... the financial statements and records. The audit for the Proteus Group, ..., ... extensive testing and review of our financial systems and controls. The other problem is that .... of Manaran statutory accounts .... the accounts we submit to Head Office.

Auditor	I can tell you one thing. The Manaran Audit report .... by our Ministry of Finance .... to renew your company's trading licence for the next year. So it is important.
MD	Oh, I see. So what will you say in your report?
Auditor	My report .... and my task was made easier thanks to the help of your accounting staff. Here's a copy for you to keep.
MD	Well, that's a relief. Have you got any other comments to make?

J Vocabulary

Useful verbs

1 Use the verbs to complete the sentences.

submit appoint perform focus involve

a) In the UK auditors may .... audits at various times of the year, depending on the date when a company publishes its annual accounts.
b) A report was .... to the Ministry of Finance.
c) The Board .... a new accountant last year.
d) The work .... a lot of detailed research into company records.
e) In his report, the engineer .... on the construction problems.

Useful noun phrases

2 Use noun phrases from the box to replace the words in italics.

auditing requirements satisfactory position financial records
head office audit layout accounting staff audit content
statutory requirements official version trading licence

a) There have been reports by several people but this is the *one which has been accepted by the board of directors.*
b) Audits have to follow *what the law says they should do.*
c) The *way the form is arranged on paper* varies from country to country.
d) There are also some differences in *what is actually included in an audit* from one country to another.
e) Before Proteus can set up in business in Barakonia, they will have to get a *special permit to carry on their business* from the Zamina Chamber of Commerce.
f) The auditor reported an *acceptable situation* when asked about his report on the annual accounts.
g) *What has to go into the audit report* should be checked by the Financial Controller.
h) A copy was sent to the *central building* of the company.
i) They examined all the *documents giving information about the finances* of the company.
j) Most of the work was done by *the people who work in the finance department of the company.*

K Grammar

Expressing compulsion

Have to ...

Most of the constructions in the Listening passage (p. 98) are in the passive. Which example below is not passive?

A The official version has to be submitted to the Ministry of Finance within the next ten days.
B .... what work has to be done for a Manaran audit.
C .... a second audit usually has to be performed by Manaran auditors.
D So we have to pay for two audits

1 Make your own examples of passive sentences from the notes.
a) A joint venture partner will .... (*find*) for the project to get off to a start.
b) Several forms .... (*fill in*) at the frontier.
c) The Protocap will .... (*show*) at exhibitions.
d) The bank .... (*persuade*) to support the project.
e) The contract .... (*sign*) last week.
f) The machinery .... (*repair*) before they could start up production again.

Before submitting it ...

Examples
A When filling in forms, I usually forget to sign them.
B After discussing finance, they talked about marketing.
C Before leaving the building, he turned off the electricity.
D On entering the country, she changed all her money.

2 Use the notes to make your own examples:

a) After (cross) the frontier, they ....
b) On (hear) the news, they ....
c) Take the pills three times a day before (eat).
d) When (drive) alone, he often ....

L Vocabulary Game

Twenty Questions

NOTE: If you have never played Twenty Questions before, or haven't played it for a long time, practise playing the ordinary version of it before playing with the vocabulary of this unit.

For each round, one person acts as the Quiz Leader. Everyone else is a Questioner. The aim of the game is to find out what the Quiz Leader has in mind by asking only 'Yes/No' type questions. The Quiz Leader is not allowed to give the answer, and can only answer the questions with 'Yes' or 'No'.

The person to guess what the Quiz Leader has in mind is the winner.
The game can be played either with the vocabulary list on page 102 in front of each player, or without looking at the list.

Annual Report and Accounts
Financial year
Forecasts
Board of Directors' report
Employment policy
Annual Accounts
Auditor's Report
Consolidated Profit and Loss Aaccount
Consolidated Balance Sheet
Cash flow statement
Statement of Accounting Policies
Share capital
Shareholders' meeting
Earnings per share
Dividends
Rationalising
Diversification
Flagship product
Earnings per share
Cash position
Notes to the Accounts
Exposure
Fluctuations
Foreign interest rates
Reported global earnings
Outward investment
Product range
Self-financing
Gearing
P/E ratio
Audit layout
Trading licence
Accounting staff

UNIT 8 Obtaining Finance

A Introduction

The story so far

While preparing to set up in an Eastern country, Proteus continued its review of its own financial position. The Group published its Annual Report and Accounts. The Chairman's report announced an 18 per cent increase in profits over the previous year and promised further rationalisation and expansion. Strong competition in Proteus's export markets was also mentioned while the Board was continuing in its search for further export markets.

Comment in the financial press was cool. It pointed out a deterioration in the Group's cash position and the danger of dependence for earnings on overseas subsidiaries. There would be problems of the risk of loss resulting from devaluation of the currencies where their subsidiaries are, and poor exchange value of their currencies.

In general, if Proteus's ambitions of expansion were to be fulfilled, more money would have to be borrowed from the bank. Profitability was not enough to generate the capital needed and it would be difficult to attract investors.

This unit is about:

a An overseas expansion strategy
b Barakonian accounting law
c Treasury management and foreign exchange risk
d Asking the bank for credit

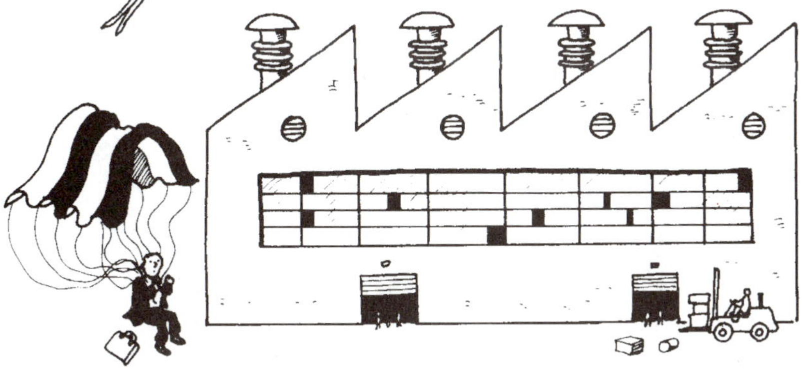

The revised ten-year strategic plan requires subsidiary companies to occupy strong and permanent positions in their principal markets.

B Reading I

Extract from a Proteus Group directive on expansion strategy

The revised ten-year strategic plan recently approved by the Proteus Group Board requires subsidiary companies to move rapidly to occupy strong and permanent positions in their principal markets. Sales should increase by 10 per cent annually and profits should grow by 15 per cent, giving a return on capital of 20 per cent for the first five years and 25 per cent for the next five years.

This expansion will be achieved through the aggressive marketing of a small range of highly profitable products, the targeting of key markets and profitable customers, a significantly higher investment in product research and development and, through the rationalisation of production facilities, to minimise fixed costs.

Proteus Manara is responsible for implementing the group's strategy in Eastern Europe. The preliminary plan has already been discussed with the Group Business Planning Department. It foresees the upgrading of manufacturing facilities in Manara and the increase of sales volumes through entry into the emerging market economies of Central and Eastern Europe.

Proteus Manara should select the country with a developing domestic economy and stable political situation, as that country could eventually serve as a base for expansion into all the major Eastern economies. ......

C Vocabulary

Adjective-noun matching

1 Read through the text again and then decide which nouns from the passage could follow the adjectives in the following groups. (*Note*: Many of the nouns used in the language of business are more often in the plural than in the singular.)

a) strategic, marketing, development, sales
b) the group, the main
c) strategic, strong, weak, leading
d) emerging, developing, growing, contracting, expanding
e) increasing, decreasing, healthy, expanding, growing, falling
f) export, targeted
g) product, wide, narrow
h) production, manufacturing
i) production, manufacturing, distribution, transport, customer
j) direct, sales, administrative, marketing, production, fixed, variable, current, manufacturing, research and development
k) marketing, sales, investment, expansion
l) market, decentralised, socialist, capitalist
m) economic, political, financial, supply

Noun-adjective matching

2 Read through the text again and then decide which adjectives from the passage could be used with the nouns in the following groups:

a) plan, data, agreement, draft, project
b) position, withdrawal, move
c) sales, forecast, economy, currency
d) improvement, presence
e) product, banks, companies, suppliers
f) advertising, selling
g) company, business, market, country, city
h) business, deal, products, customers, investment
i) industry, factor, data, information, product
j) overheads, interest, capital
k) decision, person, policy, government, company
l) draft, meeting, negotiations
m) situations, improvements, forces
n) countries, markets
o) market, airlines, problems
p) economy, conditions, relationship
q) conditions, party, factors
r) market, customer, supplier, force

Verbs

3 See how these verbs are used in the passage and use them in suitable tenses to complete the sentences below.

approve occupy give achieved target minimise serve implement foresee select

a) The plan .... a big increase in the size of the market.
b) Care should be taken .... the risks of the business.
c) The proposed investment .... an excellent return.
d) The company .... a strong position in the market.
e) Last year the company .... an 11 per cent increase in profits.
f) Several buildings were available and the directors .... one nearest their bank.
g) The scheme .... by the Ministry of Finance.
h) The letter .... as an introduction to the manager.
i) The marketing plan .... car owners.
j) They decided .... the scheme in the New Year.

Useful noun phrases

4 The words in the following phrases have been jumbled up. Put them in the right order without looking back at the text.

a) strategic year ten plan
b) Board Proteus the Group
c) on capital return

d) products profitable highly
e) and development product research
f) economies emerging the market
g) political stable situation
h) expansion for base

5 Now use the phrases from Exercise 4 and the notes below to write sentences.

a) The amount of money spent by drug companies .... is enormous.
b) They established an office in Cyprus which they wanted to use as a .... into the Middle East market.
c) The .... are experiencing major difficulties following the switch from communism.
d) The directors have decided to implement their .... which will take the firm into the next millennium.
e) The investment will produce an excellent ....
f) Following the revolutions of 1989 the rest of Europe was relieved to see a relatively .... in the former communist countries.
g) The resolution was passed at the highest level at the .... meeting last night.
h) Computer software companies have been marketing a series of .... recently.

D Grammar

Expressing obligation

1 There are various ways of expressing obligation or 'what is to be done'. Find these examples in the passage.

A (The ten year plan) .... requires subsidiary companies to move .... to occupy strong positions in their principal ....
B Proteus (Manara) is responsible for implementing the Group's strategy in Eastern Europe.

Find the following uses of 'should' in the passage. (See Unit 3, D Grammar 1 pp 33 -4 for more examples and practice of these.)

C Sales should increase by 10 per cent annually
D and profits should grow by 15 per cent giving a return on capital of 20 per cent for the first five years and 25 per cent for the next five years.
E Proteus (Manara) should select the country with a ....

'Through' used to mean 'by means of'

2 Find these examples in the passage:

This expansion will be achieved *through*
- the aggressive marketing of ....
- the targeting of ....
- a significantly higher key investment.

and *through*
- the rationalisation of production facilities.

It foresees the upgrading of manufacturing ....
and the increase of sales volumes *through*
- entry into the emerging market ....

Present perfect

3 Example of present perfect passive:
The preliminary plan *has already been discussed* with the Group Business Planning Department.

Use of prepositions

4 Choose the best preposition from the alternatives given.

a) They have a strong position / *in* / *by* / *over* / *on* / their principal markets.
b) The shareholders are looking for a good return / *for* / *to* / *on* / *by* / their capital.
c) They achieved a 50 per cent increase in sales last year / *through* / *with* / *by* / *under* / the efforts of the new Managing Director and the new sales team.
d) They decided to invest more / *in* / *with* / *for* / *into* / product research.
e) The person responsible / *over* / *by* / *with* / *for* / the department is out at lunch.
f) These problems should be discussed / *under* / *with* / *for* / *without* / all the staff concerned.
g) Their new office became a base for expansion / *towards* / *to* / *into* / *over* / the countries to the East.

Omitting 'which'

5 The revised ten-year strategic plan recently approved by the Proteus Group Board requires ....

This could also be written:

The revised ten-year strategic plan which was recently approved by the Proteus Group Board requires ....

if the writer wanted to put more emphasis on the fact that it was recently approved.

See Unit 1, F Grammar I for more about this grammar point.

E Discussion

Read the passage through again and then ask and answer questions without referring to the text.
Note: It would be useful if you made your own questions. But, if you use the questions given below, ask them in random order. It is best if you avoid answering questions by reading from the text.

What is the strategy of the Proteus Group?
What is the task of subsidiary companies?
What strategy has the Proteus Group Main Board recently approved?
What are the subsidiary companies required to do?
What annual increase in sales is expected?
What annual growth in profits is expected?
What return on capital is expected for the first five years?
What annual increase in sales is expected for the second five years?

How will the expansion be achieved?
How else?
Any other way?
What else?

What responsibilities have been assigned to Proteus Manara?
Which department of Proteus has produced the preliminary Plan?
What does the plan foresee?
How will an increase in volume of sales be achieved?

How should Proteus Manara do this?
How should Proteus Manara proceed?
What are the criteria for selecting a country as a base?

F Reading II

Extract from Barakonian accounting law

Law XVII of 1994 on Accounting
The purpose of this Law is to provide accounting regulations in line with international accounting principles, so that information can be provided which ensures a realistic and fair view of the income-generating capabilities, net assets, financial positions and future strategies of corporate entities covered by the Law.

To that end, Parliament hereby creates the following Law on Accounting:

Section 1
General Provisions

The Purpose of the Law

Paragraph 1

The Law defines the reporting and book-keeping obligations of those entities which are subject to it, the principles to be applied in the preparation of the reports and in the book-keeping, as well as the requirements relating to disclosure, publication and auditing.

The Application of the Law

Paragraph 2

(1) The Law shall apply to all participants on the market from whose operations persons and legal entities require information.

(2) The Law applies to

a) Entrepreneurs.

b) Government financed organisations.

c) Special rules will apply to the Central Bank and all registered banks.

Accounting and Book-keeping Obligations

Paragraph 14

The basic principles determined under Paragraph 15 shall be used in preparing reports and keeping the accounting records of entities. These principles will be the basis for entities to declare their accounting policies and bases and will be in line with the generally accepted accounting principles (GAAP), international accounting standards and the Directives of the European Union.

Accounting Principles

Paragraph 15

In preparing reports and in book-keeping, the assumption shall be made that the entrepreneurs shall be able to continue their operations into the foreseeable future, and that there will be no termination or significant reduction of operations for any reason (the Principle of Going Concern).

G Vocabulary

Background uses and meanings of nouns

1 Find the following nouns in the text and see how they are used. Then use them to complete the sentences.

principle	income	capabilities	provisions	obligations
disclosure	publication	directives	assumption	termination

a) The .... of 'sub judice' means that details of a criminal case before the courts of justice should not be discussed in public until the trial has ended.
b) Following the .... in the newspapers of details of the case, the judge ruled that a fair trial would be impossible.
c) The new government ministers promised to carry out their .... to their country to the best of their ability.
d) The Central Bank sometimes sends special .... to the banks telling them to reduce their lending.
e) Following the .... of the agreement, the suppliers offered a new contract.
f) .... tax is more expensive for the government to collect than indirect taxes.
g) One aim of UN policy was to remove Iraq's nuclear weapon-making ....
h) The .... of new accounting laws enabled the former communist countries to establish private enterprise.
i) The .... of the constitution of Barakonia allow for complete freedom of speech.
j) The accountancy rules are based on the .... that a company will continue trading.

Formal language

Much of the language used in this Law is formal and unlikely to be used in any other situation. You are very unlikely to need to use it, but it is useful for you to understand it. Some of the phrases can be expressed in more everyday ways.

2 How are the following ideas expressed in the text?

a) the ability to earn money (*4 words in lines 1-5*)
b) operating plans of companies (*5 words in lines 1-5*)
c) lays down the accounting laws for all companies in the country (*10 words in lines 15-20*)
d) the basic rules for the contents and presentation of company accounts (*17 words in lines 25-30*)
e) The regulations cover any business about which anyone has a right to have information (*19 words in lines 15-20*)
f) .... We are setting out fundamental rules which harmonise with those of the EC and on which companies should base their accounting procedures. (*37 words in lines 25-35*)
g) Companies which keep accounts and put out annual statements should do so on the understanding that they are going to continue in business in the same way as previously. (*one of the paragraphs*)

Less formal synonyms

3 Study how the phrases listed below are used in the text and decide which group of words each phrase belongs to.

a) application of the law
b) participants in the market
c) future strategies of corporate entities
d) income-generating capabilities
e) accounting policies and bases (GAAP)
f) the Principle of Going Concern
g) the European Union
h) entrepreneurs
i) Central Bank

i) first principles, basic assumptions, foundations
ii) business people, joint ventures, traders, merchants
iii) Brussels, Luxembourg, Strasbourg
iv) the assumption of continuing business
v) Federal Reserve Bank, Bank of England, National Bank of Hungary
vi) rules, regulations, principles, ground rules
vii) plans, schemes, moves, tactics
viii) earning, making money, accumulation of capital

H Grammar reference and practice

Purposive 'to'

1 Find examples A, B, C and D in the passage.

A The purpose of this Law is to provide accounting
B .... so that information can be provided (= *to provide information*)
C These principles will be the basis for entities to declare their ....
D .... shall be used in preparing reports and keeping the accounting ....

There is a difference in meaning between D and E:

E .. shall be used to prepare reports and keep the accounting ..

While D is integral, E is instrumental. Compare:

F They used the timber to build the house. (*instrumental*)

with

G They used their knowledge of carpentry in building the house. (*integral*)

2 How should you complete the following?:

a) The accountant used the previous year's losses .... offset this year's profits for tax purposes.
b) The accountant used cost accounting principles .... prepare the Profit and Loss Account.
c) Proteus (Manara) used the guarantee .... obtain funds from their bank.
d) .... looking for gold in the mountains, the prospector used his knowledge of geology.

Connectors

3 Study how the examples are used in the text:

A .... *in line with* international accounting principles ....
B .... *which* ensures a realistic view ....
C *To that end*, (= for that purpose ...) Parliament hereby creates ....
D .... those entities *which* are subject to it ....
E .... from *whose* operations persons and legal entities ....
F The basic principles determined under Paragraph 15 ....
Note: 'which are' is omitted from this one.

Present simple used for stating rules or acts

4 Find the following examples:

a) to that end, Parliament hereby creates
b) The Law defines the
c) The Law applies to

shall/will

5 Note that these modals are used interchangeably. The former distinction in meaning and use is dying out. In general, *shall* is used here to give more emphasis and authority.

I Discussion

Read the passage through again and then ask and answer questions about Barakonian accountancy law without referring to the text:

Note: It would be useful if you made your own questions. But if you use the questions given below, ask them in random order. It is best if you avoid answering questions by reading from the text.

What is the purpose of Law XVII of 1994 on Accounting?
What does this Law provide?
What are the accounting regulations in line with?
What is the purpose of providing accounting information?
What principles does the law follow?
Why does the law follow these principles?
What information should be provided by a business?

What else?
Anything else?
Any other information?
What is the main purpose of the new law?
What does the law define?
What obligations does it define?
What principles does it define?
What requirements does the law cover?
Whom shall the law apply to?
Why does it need to lay down rules for such organisations?
Whom in particular does the law apply to?
Anyone else?
What will the basic principles determined under Paragraph 15 be used for?
What should companies use the principles stated in the new law for?
What are the principles in line with?
Can you explain the Principle of Going Concern?

J Listening I

Discussion of treasury management and foreign exchange

The Managing Director of Proteus (Manara), the Financial Controller and the Treasury Manager from Birmingham discuss treasury management and foreign exchange. The Managing Director (MD) speaks first followed by the Treasury Manager (TM) and then the Financial Controller (FC).

Listen to the tape and complete the tapescript.

MD I've decided to sit in on your discussion because I need to understand how we should manage and report on our ....

TM Well, the present situation is that Birmingham wants you to finance your expansion through borrowing in Manara dollars.

FC I take it that means using part of these borrowings to finance our proposed investment in the East?

TM Actually .... has not yet made a decision, but you should consider borrowing either in Manara dollars or in the currency of a selected Easten country, if that's at all possible.

MD But surely the Board has already decided where we are to be funded?

TM Not entirely. Between us, some Board members are undecided about the Group's .... They fear that heavy additional borrowing will increase the Group's .... UK investors may become alarmed and sell their shares, and this would force the share price down.

FC If we invest in Manara and Eastern Europe, the assets acquired will be in the local currency and may be .... to .... if .... strengthens. So it makes sense to take out Manara dollar loans to finance these assets in order to .... or minimise possible losses. Or better still, to borrow in the country where we want to set up.

MD You mean that losses from .... into sterling will be covered in the .... by the gains when translating local currency borrowings.

FC ... and vice versa ....

HO Suppose we acquire .... in Manara for M$200,000, then at today's .... of $20 to the Pound the assets will be reported to Head Office at a value of £10,000.

MD Yes.

HO If by December 31st, when our .... ends, the exchange rate is M$25 to the pound because sterling .... the Manara dollar, the assets will be reported at £8,000.

MD A difference of £2,000 - a loss - I presume.

FC Yes, so if we borrow $200,000 to finance the purchase of assets, a loan .... as £10,000 becomes a loan of only £8,000 at the end of the year.

MD Fine, I get it. A loss of £2,000 from translating the assets is .... the gain of £2,000 when translating the loan –

FC That's why we need to persuade our Manaran bank to lend to us in dollars - and without giving them a Proteus Group .... –

MD Or an Eastern bank to lend to us in their currency.

FC That, too, seems a likely possibility.

K Vocabulary

Use of nouns

1 Find the following nouns and noun phrases in the dialogue and use them to complete the sentences.

gearing exchange losses foreign currency borrowings
long-term financing strategy local currency assets
Consolidated Balance Sheet fixed capital assets

a) The group published a .... stating the financial situation of the parent company and all its subsidiaries in one statement.
b) The board of directors had decided to avoid the risks of loss by means of .... rather than borrowing at home and exporting capital.
c) The directors of Proteus are working out a .... which will provide for financial needs in the future.
d) A fall in value of the investment currency would lead to ....
e) The .... of the company would be raised if the amount of loan capital rose in proportion to the share capital.
f) The loan was used to buy a factory site and other ....
g) .... would be translated into sterling and shown on the Balance Sheet each year.

Uses of verbs

2 The following verbs have ordinary uses. Study how they are used in a financial context in the dialogue, and decide which meaning is nearest to the one in the dialogue.

a)	minimise	i)	reduce
		ii)	eliminate completely
		iii)	make as small as possible
b)	translate	i)	show the same amount in another currency
		ii)	put into another language
		iii)	carry across from one account to another
c)	cover	i)	hide something by putting something else over it
		ii)	fill to the top
		iii)	insure
d)	strengthen	i)	make stronger
		ii)	get more valuable
		iii)	reinforce

Phrasal verbs

3 Complete the following sentences with the correct prepositions.

a) The bank's Chief Securities Clerk sat .... the meeting of the Financial Controller with the Bank Manager.
b) The accountant reported .... the financial position of the subsidiary.
c) They decided to borrow .... Deutschmarks.
d) The poor results led to selling and the share price was forced .... as a result.
e) They decided to go ahead and invest .... the joint venture.
f) She took .... a fresh life insurance policy.
g) It was a choice between setting .... a new company or buying into an existing one.
h) Last night the dollar strengthened .... the Deutschmark by 2 cents.

4 Match each of the expressions on the left with the correct explanations on the right.

a)	vice versa	i)	I understand
b)	exchange rate	ii)	the price of one currency in terms of another
c)	Between us	iii)	I am not telling this to anyone else!
d)	I get it!	iv)	the other way round
e)	I take it	v)	I assume

L Grammar

Purposive 'to'

1 Look through the tapescript and see how the following examples work.

A That means using part of these borrowings to finance our proposed investment
B .... Manara dollar loans to finance these assets ....
C .... in order to .... or minimise possible losses.

through

'Through' is used to mean 'by means of'. (See D Grammar, Exercise 2, p. 107.)

Example
Birmingham .... you .... finance your expansion .... borrowing in Manara dollars.
Birmingham want you to finance your expansion through borrowing in Manara dollars.

2 Make your own examples, using the notes.

a) The government (transform) the economy .... privatisation.
b) They (market) the product .... their sales company in Kiev.
c) Head Office (expand) into Eastern Europe .... their subsidiary in Manara.

First conditional

Note these examples in the dialogue:

A If we invest in Manara and Eastern Europe, the assets acquired will be in the local currency
B If by December 31st, when our financial year ends, the exchange rate is M$25 to the pound because sterling has strengthened against the Manara dollar, the assets will be reported at £8,000.

The use of the simple present in the main clause, implies greater certainty or the statement of a rule or law:

C If we borrow $200,000 to finance the purchase of assets, a loan initially translated as £10,000 becomes a loan of only £8,000 at the end of the year.

4 Complete the following sentences either with the future simple or the present simple, depending on whether they express greater or less certainty:

a) If interest rates fall, borrowing (increase)
b) If interest rates fall, we (borrow) more from the bank
c) Gearing (go up), if companies raise loans
d) If we borrow now, our fixed costs (increase) by a substantial amount.

persuade

5 See Unit 6, Grammar 1, p. 83, for more examples:

That's why we need to persuade our Manaran bank to lend to us in dollars - and without giving them a Proteus Group guarantee -

M Meeting

Introduction

Barakonia is a country in the East. The government, which was recently controlled by communists, has now been democratically elected and is changing the system to a market economy.

In the process of liberalisation, several Western companies and banks have been allowed to open branches or set up joint venture businesses in Barakonia. Among the foreign banks which have set up in Zamina is the Manara Lombard Bank. It was therefore to be expected that Proteus (Manara) Ltd should approach it for a loan.

Proteus (Manara) has made a formal application to the Manara Lombard Bank, Zamina branch, for a five-year loan of BD 3 million (Barakonian dinars) at a fixed rate of interest repayable in six equal monthly instalments plus interest.

Participants:

1 * The Manager of the Manara Lombard Bank, Zamina
2 The Corporate Credit Officer of the Manara Lombard Bank
3 * The Managing Director of Proteus (Manara) Ltd
4 * The Financial Controller of Proteus (Manara) ltd
5 The Marketing Manager of Proteus (Manara) Ltd
6 The Production Manager of Proteus (Manara) Ltd

The meeting should consist of at least those officials marked with an asterisk *.

Aim of the meeting:

The aim is to decide whether to provide a loan for the proposed expansion into Barakonia.

The files for each official are in the Teacher's Book.

UNIT 9 The Path to Partnership

A Introduction

The story so far

In aiming to set up in Barakonia, a country in the East, Proteus (Manara) Ltd, maker of electrical equipment, continues its review of the situation. A directive from Group Head Office emphasises the need to keep profitability in view and the management assess the principles of country risk.

The Proteus management also study sections of the accounting law of Barakonia, typical of the accounting laws recently enacted in East European countries.

Next, with the help of an expert from Head Office in Birmingham, the Managing Director and Financial Controller discuss treasury management and how to overcome the problem of foreign exchange risk to profitability of foreign investment.

Finally, in a meeting of the Proteus management with the Zamina branch of the Manara Lombard Bank, a loan was requested to finance the expansion of Proteus into Barakonia.

The Proteus management are now looking for a Barakonian partner and need to finalise the question of finance.

This unit is about:

a Auditors' reports
b Responsibility of Directors in respect of Annual Accounts
c Accounting policies of the Proteus Group plc
d Taxation and dividend regulations

The Proteus management also study sections of the accounting law of Barakonia...

B Reading I

The Auditors' Report (UK presentation)

Before reading, think about the following questions:

a) Who is the report addressed to?
b) What point in time does the report comment on?
c) What period of time does the report comment on?
d) Which two sets of rules were used to evaluate the accounts?

> To the members of Proteus Group plc:
>
> We have audited the accounts on pages 12 to 35 in accordance with Auditing Standards.
>
> In our opinion the accounts give a true and fair view of the state of affairs of the Company and the Group on December 31st 1994 and of the profit and cash flow of the Group for the financial year then ended and have been properly prepared in accordance with the Companies Act 1985.
>
> Gordon Mathieson
Chartered Accountants
Registered Auditors
>
> Birmingham
April 5th 1995

C Vocabulary

1 Find words in the report which have the same meaning as those below:

a) shareholders
b) opinion
c) situation
d) just (*adjective*)
e) law

2 Complete these sentences with phrases from the report:

a) The Proteus expansion plan was drafted (*3 words*).................... the Group directive on expansion strategy.
b) The poor (*3 words*).................... of the country's economy and the decline in exports combined to increase unemployment.
c) It takes days to ensure that everything is (*2 words*).................... for the long-distance flight of an air liner.

3 Without looking at the original passage, choose suitable words to complete the auditors' report.

To the (a).................... of Proteus Group plc:

We have (b).................... the accounts on pages 12 to 35 in (c).................... with Auditing Standards.

In our opinion (d).................... accounts give a true and fair (3).................... of the state of affairs (f).................... the Company and the Group (g).................... December 31st 1994, and of the (h).................... and cash flow of the Group (i).................... the financial year then ended and (j).................... been properly prepared in accordance (k).................... the Companies Act 1985.

D Grammar

1 How do the auditors show that they are writing to the shareholders?

2 How do the auditors show that their work is complete?

3 What does the word 'then' in the phrase 'the financial year then ended' refer to?

E Reading II

Directors' responsibilities (in respect of the preparation of the accounts)

The directors are required by company law to prepare accounts which give a true and fair view of the state of affairs of the company and of the Group at the end of the financial year and of the profit of the Group for the period up to that date. The accounts must be prepared in compliance with the required formats and rules for disclosure of the Companies Act 1985 and with the applicable accounting standards.

In addition the directors are required

* to select suitable accounting policies and apply these consistently
* to make judgements and estimates that are reasonable and prudent
* to take account of expenses and income relating to the period being reported on, whether or not they have been paid or received in that period
* to prepare the accounts on a going concern basis unless it is inappropriate to presume that the company will continue in business

The directors confirm that the accounts comply with the above requirements. They also confirm that the company has maintained adequate accounting records that ensure that the accounts comply with the requirements of the Companies Act 1985, for safeguarding the assets of the company and of the Group, and for preventing fraud and other irregularities.

F Vocabulary

1 Use adjectives from the passage to complete the following sentences.

a) Since no one knew what was going on at the branch, Head Office sent their Chief Accountant to find out the .... state of affairs.
b) The newspapers are not allowed to discuss freely a case that is before the courts, otherwise a .... trial would be impossible.
c) In some countries a first aid kit is .... equipment for a car.
d) For the movement of goods between countries, European Community regulations are ....
e) He turned up at the football match in .... clothes, having lost his kit on the train.
f) The prices are very .... at the local hotels.
g) It would be more .... to avoid spending any money until the customer has paid the deposit.
h) It would be .... to offer your doctor a cigarette when you go to consult her.
i) He could not think of an .... excuse, so he did not say anything.

2 Complete the following sentences with nouns from the passage.

a) It's important for accountants not to talk about the business .... of their customers.
b) The .... immediately after the revolution was full of optimism.
c) Manufacturers in Western Europe have to ensure the .... of their products with EC regulations.
d) Some videos are available in more than one ....
e) Following the .... of the plan to build a motorway through the oldest forest in the country, there were protests from all parties.
f) An .... was passed by parliament outlawing the sale of dangerous toys.
g) Although she was a good player, they thought she was not up to Olympic ....
h) The economic .... of the government has failed to increase employment.
i) Budget forecasts are based on .... of income and expenditure in the future.
j) He worked for an insurance .... in Vienna.
k) It's a .... of the law in the UK that every car must pass a Ministry of Transport test each year.
l) Most supermarkets have automated stock control .... nowadays.
m) Each year banks lose billions of pounds through credit card ....
n) To prevent .... in the use of cheques, banks ensure that cheques are made payable only to the account of the person named on the cheque.

3 Complete the following sentences with verbs from the text. (Sometimes the passive is required.)

a) Every student .... to pass exams from time to time.
b) A cost accountant has to decide which expenses can.......... to which income earning items.
c) It isn't always easy to see which expenses .... to which items of production.
d) The auditors .... the accounts were acceptable.
e) To .... the law every car must be insured.
f) The company .... a car for business use.
g) The company should .... that their employees are safe from fire.
h) Clean water supplies help to .... public health.
i) It's impossible to .... unemployment when fighting inflation with high interest rates.
j) The report of an earthquake in Paris has not been ....

4 How are the following ideas expressed in the text?

a) legally compulsory (*3 words, paragraph 1*)
b) have to be done according to the regulations for revealing (*13 words, paragraph 1*)
c) use them in the same way throughout (*3 words, paragraph 2*)
d) Assuming that the company is continuing in business (*5 words, paragraph 2*)
e) agree with the rules just described (*5 words, paragraph 3*)

5 Without looking back at the reading passage, complete the text using the appropriate verbs. (Use a suitable verb tense. Sometimes a passive is needed.)

The directors (a).................... by company law to (b).................... accounts which (c).................... a true and fair view of the state of affairs of the company[...] The accounts must (d) .... in compliance with the required formats and rules for disclosure [...]

In addition the directors are required

- (e).................... suitable accounting policies and (f).................... these consistently

- (g).................... judgements and estimates that are reasonable and prudent

- (h, 4 words).................... expenses and income (i).................... to the period being reported on, [...]

- to prepare the accounts on a going concern basis unless it is inappropriate (j).................... that the company will continue in business

The directors (k).................... that the accounts (l).................... with the above requirements. They also confirm that the company (m).................... adequate accounting records that (n).................... that the accounts comply with the requirements of the Companies Act 1985, for (o).................... the assets of the company and of the Group, and for (p).................... fraud and other irregularities.

G Grammar

The passive

Note the following examples:

A The directors *are required by company law* to prepare..........
B The accounts *must be prepared* in compliance with ....
C income relating to the period *being reported* on ....

The passive is used in formal English to express obligation, and to avoid mention of the subject:

1 Now rewrite the words in italics in the following sentences, using the passive.

a) The directors confirm that .... *comply with the above requirements.*
b) They also confirm that .... *has maintained adequate accounting records*
c) and that .... *comply with the requirements of the Companies Act 1985.*
d) It is important that .... *should prevent fraud and other irregularities.*
e) They also have to ensure that .... *conform to EC regulations.*
f) When preparing accounts .... *must observe certain rules.*

Relative clauses

Example
The directors are required by company law to prepare accounts *which* give a true and fair view of the state of affairs of the company ....

2 Join the following pairs of sentences in the same way.

a) They have to follow rules.
+ The rules concern the preparation of accounts.
b) The directors select the accounting policies.
+ The accounting policies suit the needs of the company.
c) They must take account of the income and expenses.
+ The income and expenses relate to the period being reported on.
d) The directors also confirm that the company has maintained accounting records.
+ The accounting records ensure that the accounts comply with the requirements of the Companies Act 1985.
e) They must also have records.
+ The records safeguard the assets of the company and of the group.

Reported actions

3 Compare the following examples A and B (from the text) with C and D.

A The directors confirm that the accounts comply with the above requirements.
B They also confirm that the company has maintained adequate accounting records.

C The directors confirmed that the accounts complied with the above requirements.
D They also confirmed that the company had maintained adequate accounting records.

What rule can you make from this comparison?

4 Now apply the rule you have deduced to put the verbs in brackets into the correct tenses

a) The directors state that the accounts (give) a true and fair view of the state of affairs of the company.
b) The auditors reported that the accounts (prepare) in compliance with the required formats and rules for disclosure of the Companies Act 1985 and with the applicable accounting standards.
c) In addition the directors assure the shareholders that suitable accounting policies (select) and (apply) consistently.
d) They say that all their judgements and estimates (be) reasonable and prudent.
e) The directors confirm that all expenses and income relating to the period being reported on, whether or not they have been paid or received in that period (account for).
f) They also state that the accounts (prepare) on a going concern basis.

H Discussion

Ask and answer questions on Reading I and II.

Who is the auditors' report addressed to?
What does the auditors' report report on?
What else does the auditors' report report on?
Anything else?
What standards are referred to?
What other rules are referred to?

What are the responsibilities of the directors of a company in respect of the preparation of the accounts?

What other responsibilities do they have?
What others?
What else?
Anything else?

Why do the directors have to do these things?
What sort of view of the state of affairs of the company do they have to provide?
What period do the accounts cover?
How should the accounts be prepared?
What rules should they take into account?
What other requirements must the annual accounts take into account?
What else?
Anything else?
What should the accounting records ensure?
What is the purpose of the Companies Act 1985?
Any other purpose?
Anything else?

I Reading III

Extract from Accounting Policies of Proteus Group plc

1 *Basis of Preparation of Accounts*
The accounts are prepared under the historical cost convention and comply with all applicable UK accounting standards. The accounts incorporate the audited assets and liabilities of subsidiary companies and the Group's share of associated companies for the year.

2 *Turnover*
Turnover is goods and services invoiced during the year to external customers and associated companies, excluding value added tax and other sales taxes, less trade discounts.

3 *Foreign Currencies*
Foreign currency assets and liabilities, including those of overseas subsidiary and associated companies are translated into sterling at rates of exchange ruling on Balance Sheet date. The results of overseas subsidiary and associated companies are translated using average rates of exchange.

Exchange adjustments arising directly from the translation of Balance Sheet items are taken directly to reserves. All other exchange differences are included in the Profit and Loss Account.

4 *Fixed Assets*
Tangible fixed assets are carried at cost less depreciation. Depreciation is normally calculated so as to write-off the cost of fixed assets (except freehold land) evenly over their estimated useful lives. Estimated useful lives are reviewed periodically, taking into account commercial and technological obsolescence as well as normal wear and tear.

For the normally expected lives of the major categories of fixed assets, see the Glossary under **Fixed assets**.

5 *Research and Development*

Research and development expenditure, other than on fixed assets, is treated as a charge against revenue in the year in which it is spent.

6 *Stocks*

Stocks are included in the accounts either at cost (including manufacturing overheads, where appropriate) or net realisable value, whichever is the lower.

J Vocabulary

(*Note*: Many of the words occurring in Reading III may have occurred in earlier readings and so been dealt with in vocabulary work. Use the Index to look up words used earlier in the course.)

1 How are the following ideas expressed in the text?

a) The custom of valuing something at its original price (*3 words, paragraph 1*)
b) The rules which have a bearing on (*4 words, paragraph 1*)
c) Another business which works together with one's own business on some joint project (*2 words, paragraph 1*)
d) People who buy things from you and are not one of your subsidiary companies (*2 words, paragraph 2*)
e) A figure expressed in a different currency (*3 words, paragraph 3*)
f) The annual accounts (*2 words, paragraph 3*)
g) The value of one currency in terms of another (*3 words, paragraph 3*)
h) Gains or losses resulting from changes in the exchange rate (*2 words, paragraph 3*)
i) Surplus money or profits which are shown in the Balance Sheet separately from capital (*1 word, paragraph 3*)
j) A progressive reduction in value resulting from wear and tear, obsolescence or market change (*1 word, paragraph 4*)
k) The act of reducing the value of something until it has no accountable value at all (*1 word, paragraph 4*)
l) The suggested length of life of an asset (*3 words, paragraph 4*)

2 Use appropriate verbs from the box to complete the sentences.

incorporate	carry at cost	write off	review	treat as
to be included in				

a) The newspaper .... the market every day.
b) They decided to .... the death .... a murder.
c) The partnership .... as a public limited company in1988.

d) The office furniture and equipment .... under fixed assets.
e) At the end of its useful life the equipment ....
f) The accountant decided to .... the computer equipment .... current assets.

3 Allocate a suitable adjective from the text to each group of nouns.

Paragraph 1

a) cost, data, precedant, character
b) rules, regulations, law, principles, criteria
   (*3 possibilities*)
c) assets, liabilities
d) company, organisation, business, firm, concern
   (*2 possibilities*)

Paragraph 2

e) goods, services, supplies
f) customers, accounts, affairs, services
g) figures, tax, force, effort, conference, meeting
h) discount, figures, finance, embargo, journal, publication, rebate

Paragraph 3

i) currency, country, goods, language, affairs, travel
j) subsidiary, investment, travel, contracts, contacts
k) figures, performance, earnings, yield, output, sales, income

Paragraph 4

l) sum, payment, assets, liabilities
m) benefits, assets, results, figure
n) figure, cost, need, requirement, output, production
o) bank, activity, success, traffic
p) changes, improvements, advances, superiority, age, society
q) categories, changes, improvements, benefit,

Paragraph 6

r) profit, result, improvement, importer, exporter
s) assets, value

4 Match the nouns on the left with their explanations on the right.

convention	percentage reduction
standards	completely owned property
turnover	becoming out-of-date
discount	deterioration through use
depreciation	custom
freehold	annual income
obsolescence	measure of quality
wear and tear	rebate

K Grammar

Use of prepositions

Complete the following sentences with the best choice of preposition.

a) The agreement was drawn up / *with* / *by* / *along* / *under* / agreed international accounting rules.
b) The accounts comply / *with* / *to* / *by* / *under* / the rules for preparing accounts.
c) The figure was translated / *in* / *to* / *into* / *over*/ sterling in the consolidated accounts for the group.
d) They changed the money / *with* / *by* / *under* / *at* / a very favourable rate.
e) Expenses arising directly / *out of* / *from* / *in* / *with* / production are included with overheads.
f) The figure was carried / *by* / *with* / *at* / *under* / cost less depreciation.
g) Depreciation is normally calculated so as to write off assets evenly /*throughout* / *during* / *over* / *before* / their estimated useful lives.

L Discussion

Ask and answer questions with a partner.

What is the basis of preparation of accounts?
What convention are the accounts prepared under?
What is the historical cost convention?
What do the accounts of a group of companies incorporate?
What is turnover?
What is excluded from turnover?
How are foreign currency assets and liabilities shown in the balance sheet?
How are the results of overseas subsidiary and associated companies translated?
How are exchange adjustments dealt with?
How are tangible fixed assets handled?
How is depreciation normally applied?
What is taken into account when calculating the useful life of an asset?
How is research and development expenditure treated?
How are stocks treated?

M Listening I

Taxation and dividends

The Financial Controller (FC), a Barakonian accountant (BA) and the Accounts Manager from the Birmingham office (AM), discuss taxation and dividends in Manara and Barakonia at the Proteus office in Manara City. Listen to the tape and complete the dialogue.

FC How are things in Barakonia? Is what I've heard true that the liberalisation process is extending to the tax system?

BA Regrettably not, I'm afraid. The government is keeping an iron grip on the economy by a heavy burden of .... individuals and companies. But ...., such as .... and .... have been avoided.

AM I know what you mean. The ...., in his .... has just increased taxation all round.

FC Well, in Manara we seem to have the best of all worlds. We have .... either Barakonia or the UK. Also it's .... to foreign .... But it's not all a bed of roses. VAT is going up and there are going to be ...., petrol and tobacco.

BA What about ....?

FC The .... is coming down from 40 per cent to 35 per cent but the first 100,000 .... are taxed at 25 per cent and there's an allowance for training.

AM Yes, I think the authorities here are going in the right direction. But what interests us most at the moment is ....

BA Well, in Barakonia no dividends .... to foreign shareholders for the first three years of an investment. Thereafter dividends .... and are .... of 5 per cent.

FC In Manara it's 10 per cent from the outset. But companies which withdraw invested capital within five years of when it was invested .... of the total remitted.

..........Ah, here's the coffee and some Schplugotonic water from Barakonia[...]

N Vocabulary

1 How are the following ideas expressed in the dialogue?

a) Changes which are freeing the economy from restrictions (*2 words*)
b) A tight control (*3 words*)
c) The British finance minister (*2 words*)
d) Send profits (*2 words*)
e) Not everything is wonderful (*7 words*)
f) The government is doing the right thing (*9 words*)
g) Profits returned to the country from which the original investment came (*2 words*)
h) A tax on dividends sent out of the country (*2 words*)

Different kinds of tax

2 Complete the sentences, using the right tax phrase.

penalty	sales	corporation	withholding	value added

a) .... tax is added on to the price of items sold by retailers.
b) Among the firm's current liabilities was a figure for .... tax which is calculated as a percentage of its selling price.
c) Every time a service or a product is sold on it attracts .... tax which is calculated as a percentage of its selling price.
d) Many countries charge a .... tax on dividends when they are paid to the original foreign investor.
e) If the company pulled out of Manara now, it would have to pay out the 5 per cent .... tax on its capital.

3 Replace the words in italics with more suitable expressions from the box.

repatriate	an allowance
subject to	Autumn Budget
special duties	luxury goods
standard rate	withdraw capital

a) If Proteus *brings money back* from Barakonia within five years, it will lose on the investment.
b) To encourage foreign investment governments usually make it easy to *send* profits *back*.
c) In his *half-yearly statement of government finances* the Minister explained the new taxes.
d) Certain kinds of expenditure are classified as *permitted expenses* which may be offset against tax.
e) Profits are *liable to* income tax at varying rates.
f) Sometimes governments raise extra money by imposing *extra taxes* on particular items.
g) What's the *basic calculation* for tax in your country?
h) Sometimes it is felt that *expensive goods which are not necessary for living* are a suitable subject of taxation.

O Listening II

The Financial Controller (FC), the Barakonian Accountant (BA) and the Accounts Manager (AM) continue their conversation about tax and dividends in Manara and Barakonia.

BA Hmm. You've got a good brand of Schplugotonic, I see. As I was saying, the taxation situation in Barakonia is not very encouraging to foreign investors.

FC Oh dear. What about ....?

BA Yes, I was coming to that. You see the government has to featherbed all the Barakonians who are not accustomed to unemployment by ensuring good .... and ensuring that all employers pay their ....

AM I suppose that leads to firms employing as few people as possible and .... as much of .... as possible ....

BA That's right. And .... are .... For example, allowances on fixed capital assets allows plant to be depreciated.......... .... There are no exceptions and .... charges are not .... expenses.

FC What about remitting dividends on investments?

BA As I mentioned before, you can't remit anything for three years from the date of investment. You have to ....

AM So, what you're saying is, if we put money into Barakonia it has to be a long-term investment and we won't expect to .... years.

BA Yes, that's quite right.

FC So it's not surprising Birmingham won't help us and we will have to finance any Barakonian venture out of after-tax profits from Manara. There will be no dividends to pay to Birmingham and so no .... Another advantage for us is that Manaran tax law allows us to .... over ten years.

P Vocabulary

1 How are the following ideas expressed in the dialogue?

a) The Barakonian government offers no incentives to people from abroad wishing to put money into the country. *(12 words)*
b) Protect people who are not used to having no jobs *(10 words)*
c) Firing as many people as possible from their jobs *(9 words)*
d) Some spending by companies may not be offset against tax. *(6 words)*
e) Depreciation calculated by dividing the value of the asset by the number of years of its useful life *(6 words)*
f) Sending back profits on capital *(4 words)*
g) Don't expect to get any money back for several years. *(8 words)*
h) Depreciation based on a percentage of the remaining balance each year after subtracting the depreciation of the previous year *(4 words)*

Q Vocabulary Game

Write down all the words in the lists below on pieces of paper or card. Write a number on each pair of cards to ensure that they can be matched. Place all the column B papers face down on the table and deal out the remainder to the group. The aim is to collect the most pairs.

Column 1 A	Column 1 B	Column 2 A	Column 2 B
tax	system	invested	capital
indirect	tax	penalty	tax
sales	tax	social	security
value added	tax	unemployment	benefit
remit	dividends	social	insurance
foreign	investors	workforce	redundancy
luxury	goods	business	expenses
corporation	tax	tax-deductible	expenses
standard	rate	straight line	depreciation
training	allowance	long term	view
repatriated	dividends	after-tax	profits
withholding	tax	reducing balance	depreciation

UNIT 10 Deciding on Partners

A Introduction

The story so far

Unit 9 explained further accounting information needed by Proteus, the electrical manufacturer of Manara, and any prospective partner in Barakonia.

The Auditors' Report is an important document accompanying the Proteus Group annual accounts because it verifies that the published financial information gives a true and fair view of the Group including its subsidiaries which, in this case, includes Proteus (Manara).

There then follows a textbook statement of the directors' responsibilities in a public company to prepare annual accounts in accordance with the law and accounting convention. Thus, by reading the published annual accounts, prospective investors or partners should be able to have a true and clear view of the company they are about to invest in or join.

There then follows a description of the accounting policies of the Proteus Group. These are a list of rules which make it possible for the accountants preparing financial documents for the company to follow varying procedures in harmony with each other.

Finally there is a discussion between the Financial Controller of Manara, the Accounts Manager from Birmingham and a Barakonian accountant on taxation and rules for inward investment in Manara and Barakonia.

This unit is about:

a The Proteus Business Plan
b Choosing a business partner
c The Proteus Financial Controller's report on Elektra, a possible joint venture partner

Choosing a business partner...

B Reading I

The Proteus Manara Business Plan 1995–8

1 *Mission objectives*

We aim to establish a permanent, dominant position in the major markets of Central and Eastern Europe. We will concentrate on high-value products which generate high profit margins and which have a potential for extensive value added services in the areas of maintenance, training and development.

We shall apply the technology developed by our UK research and development laboratory to low-cost manufacturing in Barakonia. We shall set up a system under our control for distributing Proteus products through joint-venture organisations, subsidiary companies or exclusive distributorships. These may be in Barakonia or in neighbouring countries.

Through rigorous selection of suppliers, we shall increase local sourcing of key materials. Through intensive and continuous training we shall develop local managerial and technical skills in order to reduce labour costs and the dependence on 'imported' expertise.

2 *Long-term aims*

To achieve a 30 per cent share of each key market by 1998 and an increase in after-tax profits of 17 per cent of sales and return on capital employed of 20 per cent.

To obtain full management control of the Proteus operation in each key market (where a dominant position is attainable) within 3 - 5 years;

To establish exclusive distributorships in markets judged to be of substantial future potential, and to appoint agents in all other markets.

To increase the degree of 'nationalisation' of all products through increasing proportion of locally sourced or manufactured materials from 20 per cent to 50 per cent of the total manufacturing cost.

C Vocabulary

Verbs

1 Use verbs from the box to complete the sentences. Use a suitable tense. Sometimes you may need to use the passive.

source	obtain	generate	establish	distribute
develop	concentrate on	appoint	aim	achieve

a) The Proteus Group .... to set up a joint venture company in Barakonia.
b) Once the company has been .... they will set up local manufacturing.
c) Although they make all kinds of domestic electrical goods, they .... capital goods in the new market.
d) They will have to .... enough income to meet their targeted return on capital employed.

e) The Protocap .... by the Proteus Group and made by their subsidiary in Manara.
f) The car makers decided to .... their components in the Czech Republic.
g) When a film is released, it .... to cinemas everywhere.
h) They .... excellent sales in the first six months.
i) When Proteus took Pifco over, they .... control of all the Pifco brand names.
j) Poptek .... Managing Director in Barakonia.

Nouns

2 Use the clues to decide which noun from the list best fits the sentence.

technology	sourcing	selection	potential	objectives	mission
maintenance	laboratory	expertise	distributorships	development	

a) They have a .... in Bosnia.
Clues: being sent to do a task, going somewhere to do something
b) The governments of the two countries have similar economic ....
Clue: We have these in mind when planning our life and work.
c) There is considerable .... in the Barakonian market.
Clue: There isn't much now but great things will come later.
d) Machine .... is a factory overhead.
Clue: Airline companies must be extremely careful about this.
e) They spend money on research and .... to ensure the future growth of the company.
Clue: growing, expanding, becoming mature, evolving.
f) Archimedes showed the general how to use .... in defence of the city.
Clue: Branches of applied science make work more efficient.
g) The product won't be ready for a long time. It's still at .... stage.
Clue: a room where research takes place, where scientists work.
h) They made a .... from a wide range of products.
Clue: choice
i) Like technology, ... is transferable across frontiers and becomes part of the ability of the importing country.
Clue: People who are very good at what they do provide this.
j) The company's .... of components follows a policy of most reliable supplier.
Clue: You do this when you find where you can obtain something.
k) They established .... in each country where their products had a market.
Clue: You must be good at selling things all over your area if you want this.

Adjectives

This exercise is designed to help you to know which adjectives are used with which nouns.

3 Use the clues to assign a suitable adjective from the box to each of the following lists of nouns. (More than one adjective may be possible in many cases.)

substantial	rigorous	permanent	neighbouring	managerial	major
long-term	local key	intensive	high value	extensive	exclusive
dominant	continuous				

a) feature, improvement, disability, relationship, union, separation, system
Clue: Things which can last a very long time
b) position, partner, country, product, brand, role
Clue: Something which can be stronger or bigger
c) influence, player, force
Clue: Something which can be very important
d) products, contracts, goods, deals, bank notes, bills
Clue: Things which can be worth a lot
e) damage
f) distributorship, agent, club, clientele, deal, agreement
Clue: Something which can not allow anyone else to have a share
g) country, factory, forest, garden, park, building
Clue: Something that can be next to your house
h) selection, examination, test, criteria, interview
Clue: Something that is very tough or strict
i) shops, cinema, post office, government, currency, sourcing
Clue: Something near you or in the country where you do business
j) fact, figure, word, expression, market, materials
Clue: things which are of central importance
k) training, study, research, investigation
Clue: Something done by students, policy, committees
l) training, study, research, investigation, service, support, help
Clue: Things which go on and on and on
m) Skills, training, decisions, meetings
Clue: Things which those in charge must have or make
n) improvement, contract, loan, credit, decision, policy
Clue: Things which will last for some time into the future
o) sum, help, figure, savings, costs, amounts, increase, fall
Clue: Things which can be very large

Linked words

4 Without looking at the passage, improve the following sentences by replacing the words in italics with words from the passage.

a) Toyota have established a *superior place* in the Asian car market. (*2 words, paragraph 1*)
b) They want to *make a lot of money* in Barakonia. (*4 words, paragraph 1*)
c) They want to sell products which lock the customer into *expensive after-sales services.* (*12 words, paragraph 1*)
d) They want to use *cheap labour* in Barakonia. (*3 words, paragraph 2*)
e) Proteus will set up *their own firms* in Barakonia. (*2 words, paragraph 2*)
f) They will use *carefully worked-out methods of choosing* suppliers. (*2 words, paragraph 3*)
g) Many multinational companies *obtain more and more of their most important supplies for manufacturing in the host country.* (*6 words, paragraph 3*)
h) They *build up the work-force of a subsidiary from host country nationals so as to lower the cost of using more expensive workers from the country of the parent company.* (*18 words, paragraph 3*)
i) They want to establish themselves first in the *area where they can sell most.* (*2 words, paragraph 4*)
j) The company will concentrate on the countries which have *the best prospects for growth.* (*4 words, paragraph 5*)

5 Without referring back to Reading I, match the words from the column on the left with words from the column on the right to make phrases from the reading passage.

a permanent	skills
exclusive	products
high value	potential
key	position
labour	markets
low-cost	manufacturing
neighbouring	distributorship
subsidiary	countries
substantial	costs
technical	companies

D Grammar

Purposive 'to'

Example
We aim to establish .... (*line 1*)

1 Find a three-word example of a purposive conjunction in paragraph 3.

a) In what way are the following examples not complete sentences? How could you complete them?

To achieve a 30 per cent share of each key market by 1995 and .... an increase in after tax profits of 17 per cent of sales and .... a return on capital employed of 20 per cent

b) Now find other examples of the same kind of 'non-sentences'.

Will/shall

Both *will* and *shall* indicate the future. But one of them is a simple expression of the future and the other is more an expression of intention. Which is which?

2 Find these examples in the passage:

A We will concentrate on ...
B We shall apply the technology developed by our UK research and development laboratory to ...
C ... we shall increase local sourcing of key materials.
D ... we shall develop local managerial and technical skills in order to reduce ...

3 Find a word which means 'by means of'.

E Before reading

Read the Introduction to the Financial Controller's Report below and answer the questions.

> This report was written for the Proteus Head Office Finance Department by the Manara Financial Controller after his visit to Elektra Ltd, of Zamina, in Barakonia.
>
> 'I spent one day with the staff of the Accounting Department of Elektra Ltd in Zamina and concluded that if Proteus acquires control, then a reorganisation of this department will be essential, followed by re-training at all levels.'

a) Who was the report written for?
b) The Financial Controller of which company wrote the report?
c) What was the reason for his visit to Elektra?
d) Why did he recommend that a reorganisation of the accounts department of Elektra was necessary?

F Reading II

Extract from the Financial Controller's Report

1 *Organisation and staffing*
Elektra's accounting department is headed by the Chief Accountant who reports to the General Manager. It has four sections: Financial Accounting, Payroll, Industrial Costing and Inventory Control. The section heads have excellent experience of their own sections, but little knowledge of the work of the others.

The Payroll, Costing, Personal Accounts and Inventory systems are run on a small minicomputer, while the Central Accounting System is run manually, as no software is available to process data from the minicomputer without re-entry of data.

2 *Background*
The company follows the system laid down by National Accounting Law No. 420 issued in 1980, which requires companies of the size of Elektra to maintain a double entry system and prescribes in great detail what accounts should be used and what reports should be submitted.

All companies must end their financial year on December 31st. Until 1989, most reports were sent either to the Barakonian Central Planning Department or the National Statistics Office.

G Vocabulary

1 Replace the words in italics with expressions from the reading passage which have the same meaning. (Sometimes the sentence must be rewritten.)

a) The management was *led* by Mr Pivotski. (*1 word, paragraph 1*)
b) Mr Pivotski *is accountable* to the Board of Directors. (*1 word, paragraph 1*)
c) They have *learnt a great deal through their work.* (*3 words, paragraph 1*)
d) For most of its flight the jet is flown and navigated by computers, but for landing and take-off it is flown *by the pilot.* (*1 word, paragraph 2*)
e) If the files are destroyed, *putting all the information into the records again* will be necessary. (*3 words, paragraph 2*)
f) New accounting rules were *brought in* by the government. (*2 words, paragraph 3*)
g) The law *lays down* compulsory insurance for all car owners. (*1 word, paragraph 3*)

Word families

2 Choose words and phrases from the box which are related to each of the words below.

workers	staffing	re-entry	recruitment	programme
processor	personnel	mini-computer	management	figures
distribution	systems	data	average	application

a) staffing
b) software
c) statistics

3 Now find words relating in the same way to the following:

a) Organisation (*2 words in paragraph 1; 1 word in paragraph 2; 3 words in paragraph 4*)
b) headed by (*3 three-word phrases in paragraph 1; a verb in paragraph 2*)
c) laid down (*1 noun and 4 verbs in paragraph 3; one verb in paragraph 4*)

H Reading III

The Proteus Financial Controller's report on Elektra's accounting system (continued)

3 *Presentation of accounting information*
The mandatory format for the Balance Sheet and Profit Statement is of limited use for management control purposes. But although the industrial costing section collects detailed information on unit costs, it is not presented in a way to facilitate decisions on selling prices, which were previously set by the Barakonian Central Planning Agency.

The company maintains a system of Day Books whose results are summarised into Personal Accounts for customers' and suppliers' accounts – similar to the UK Sales and Purchase Ledgers. Summarised data is transferred each month to a Central Accounting Book, which is equivalent to the UK Nominal or General Ledger, and from which monthly trial balances are produced.

4 Auditing and internal control

An annual audit is carried out by the Chief Accountant of a neighbouring company during a one-week period in March. It amounts to little more than a desk review of the statutory financial reports to ensure their compliance with the law. There is no formal audit according to UK or international standards, although there is some internal control activity. The Inventory Control section personally carry out checks on levels of stock items which are critical to the achievement of production targets. The Payroll Department checks its own records each month to ensure that wages are correctly computed and that all taxes are collected and paid over to the Tax Office.

I Vocabulary

1 Select the most suitable verb from the box to complete each of the following sentences. (You may have to use an auxiliary verb to complete the sense.)

transfer	summarise	set	produce	pay over	amounts to	achieve
maintain	ensure	compute	collect	check	facilitate	carry out

a) The Sales Manager and the Chief Accountant .... the firm's selling prices every six months.
b) The factory .... a system of computerised stock control in all its retail outlets.
c) The results of the government's statistical research .... in a booklet published by Her Majesty's Stationery Office each year.
d) Billions of bits of data .... by fibre optic technology.
e) An interim Balance Sheet .... every six months.
f) Audits .... annually.
g) The report .... a confirmation of what I have been saying for weeks.
h) Customs checks at the frontier .... that smuggling is kept to a minimum.
i) The bank's internal auditors .... audits round the year.
j) The sales department was pleased to .... the sales required by the business plan.
k) The stock records .... every month to make sure they are accurate.
l) The programme is designed .... the social security and national health contributions and income tax of each employee.
m) Value added tax is a cheap way of .... taxes because it is partly self-administered.
n) The Tennis Club Secretary had receipts which showed that all the money she had collected .... to the Treasurer.
o) The information collected by Customs .... government decisions on import taxation.

2 Complete the sentences using the best alternative adjective:

a) An accounting format that is required by law is a / *compulsory* / *legal* / *mandatory* / *obligatory* / format.
b) The information produced by the Department of Trade is of /*minimal* / *limited* / *restricted* / use for planning our project.
c) Data needed to enable managers to run a business are used for management / *command* / *control* / *orders* / *purposes.*
d) Financial data used by management is called / *accounting* / *accountancy* / *account* / *accountant* / information.
e) Much of the data was too general. They wanted more / *specific* / *accurate* / *correct* / *detailed* / information.
f) The / *summarised* / *collected* / *summary* / *assumed* / data is produced from figures collected by the Ministry.
g) / *Interior* / *Interim* / *Infernal* / *Internal* / financial control is provided by the accounts department.
h) Reports required by law are / *statuary* / *stationary* / *statutory* / *stationery* / reports.
i) Each year a company must have / *a former* / *a formal* / *an official* / *an informal* / audit carried out.
j) The report was written by the / *chef* / *head* / *chief* /accountant.
k) The / *angular* / *annual* / *annular* / *angle* / audit was carried out by Krakpot Chekit & Co.
l) A minimum sale of seventy thousand in the first year is / *cruel* / *crucial* / *critical* / *essential* / to the achievement of success.

3 Complete the following terms.

a) Balance ....
b) Profit ....
c) The industrial .... section
d) .... costs
e) .... Books
f) Sales and .... ledgers
g) .... Accounting Book
h) Nominal or .... Ledger
i) Monthly trial ....
j) Auditing and .... Control
k) .... review
l) Statutory .... reports

J Grammar

The passive

1 Look at the following examples of the use of the passive:

A Elektra's accounting department *is headed by* the Chief Accountant
B The Payroll .... systems *are run* on a small minicomputer ...
C ... while the Central Accounting System *is run* manually ...
D The company follows the system *laid down* by National Accounting Law No. 420 issued in 1980.

E what accounts *should be used* and
F what reports *should be submitted.*
G Most reports *were sent* either to ....
H Detailed information on unit costs *is not presented* in a way to facilitate decisions ...
I Summarised data *is transferred* each month to a Central Accounting Book ...
J An annual audit *is carried out* by the Chief Accountant of ..
K .... that wages *are* correctly *computed* and ....
L ... that all taxes *are collected and paid over* to the Tax Office.

Now match each of the examples with Type 1, Type 2 or Type 3 below.

1 The identity of the agent (the person who did the action) is unimportant or irrelevant: e.g. Thousands of ugly buildings were put up all over England in the 1960s.
2 The writer wishes to focus on the object of the action rather than the subject performing the action: e.g. The dog was bitten by the man.
3 Combination of 1 and 2

There are/it has

2 Why use *It has* instead of *There are/is*?

Note these examples taken from Reading II:

A It has four sections: Financial Accounting, Payroll ....
which could be written:
There are four sections (etc.)
B as no software is available.
which could be written:
as they have no available software
C There is no formal audit according to UK .... standards. (Elektra has no formal audit ....)
D .... there is some internal control activity. (The company has some internal ....)

Softening negative comment

3 Note this use of *little*, taken from Reading II:

A (they have) *little knowledge* of the work of the others.
= They know hardly anything at all about the work of the others.

and compare it with:

B They have *a little knowledge* of the work of the others.
= They do know something about the others' work.

Which of these two sentences is less harsh?
Find the example in Reading III.

Note also:

C He has few friends. (i.e. not many)
D He has a few friends in high places. (i.e. 'quite a lot')
E He'd had a few beers. (i.e. He was somewhat drunk.)

While/as

4 Both of these conjunctions can sometimes mean 'because' and sometimes mean 'at the same time'. Decide which meaning is intended in the examples here. (See p. 98 for more examples.)

A .... while the Central Accounting System is run manually....
B .... as no software is available to process data from .....

Either/or

5 Note the example:

–.... either to the Barakonian Central Planning Department or the National Statistics Office.

Which meaning does this convey?

a) The writer doesn't know whether they sent the figures to the Barakonian Central Planning Department or the National Statistics Office.
b) The writer knows but he has chosen not to say which.
c) It isn't important anyway.

K Discussion

The following questions should be discussed without looking at the original reading passages. Read them through again before starting the discussion.

Ask and answer:

Who heads Elektra's Accounting Department?
What are the sections of the accounting department?
What was the Financial Controller's comment on the section heads?
What sort of equipment does Elektra's accounting department have?
Why is the central accounting system run manually?
What sort of controls were in operation?
When does the Barakonian financial year end?
Is this the case in Western countries? (See p. 89, paragraph 1.)
What happens to most reports?
What problem is posed by the way information about unit costs is presented?
In what way did the setting of prices differ from the way they are set in Western companies?
What is produced from the Day Books?
Where is all the information collected?
What is the UK equivalent to the Central Accounting Book?
What is derived from Central Accounting Book?
Who carried out Elektra's annual audit?
What does the Financial Controller say about the annual audit?
What else does he say?
What sort of controls does Elektra operate?
How do they ensure that wages are correctly computed and that all taxes are collected and paid over to the Tax Office?

L Dialogue

The Proteus Financial Controller (FC), Production Manager (PM) and Marketing Manager (MM) discuss the costing of the Protocap Energy Saver.

Listen to the tape and complete the tapescript.

FC If you look at the .... for the Energy Saver you can see that the .... does not fall when sales increase towards the end of 1994.

PM Yes, that's amazing. Even if my planned reorganisation of production methods reduces total labour time on the Energy Saver from 5.6 to 4.5 hours by 1996, the .... as a percentage of sales will remain around 63 per cent. So what's happening and what can we do?

FC Well at present we have to buy all the main .... from our factory in Birmingham - that's group policy. It also helps to .... to the UK through .... the .... We also have to pay the .... which add about 10 per cent to the.......... ....

MM We also have to absorb any ....

PM Yes. But we can cut costs by finding local suppliers for as many sub-assemblies as possible.

MM That's fine. But how can we be sure of the .... of locally produced assemblies?

PM That's my job. It'll be tricky but there's no point in ignoring .... wherever possible. Otherwise we'll lose one of the main advantages of producing in Barakonia. Another one is the faster production rate over there. What was it?

FC It'll take the Barakonia plant, once it's going, 50 minutes less than the factory in Manara to make the Energy Saver. That'll bring down the .... costs and the.......... .... even after we have revised our present allocation methods to take in the cost of .... in the .... and ....

MM All this should enable me to set a ....

FC That should bring in a substantial increase in sales which will in turn reduce .... Our .... and .... will be .... over a greater number of ....

M The meeting

Introduction:
Barakonia is a country in the East. The government, which was recently controlled by communists, has now been democratically elected and is changing the system to a market economy.

In the process of liberalisation, several Western companies have been allowed to open branches or set up joint venture businesses in Barakonia. Proteus (Manara) Ltd, the electrical subsidiary of the Proteus Group plc, has contacted two Barakon companies – Elektra Ltd in Zamina, the capital, and Astra of Damadossa.

The meeting which you are going to simulate is the one with Elektra Ltd.

Participants:
Electra Ltd

1 The General Manager *
2 The Chief Accountant *
3 The Secretary to the Works Council
4 Financial Adviser

Proteus (Manara) Ltd

3 The Managing Director *
4 The Financial Controller *
5 The Marketing Manager

The meeting should consist of at least those officials marked with an asterisk.

Aims of the Meeting:
Elektra must decide whether or not to form the partnership with Proteus.
Proteus must decide whether or not to form the partnership with Elektra.

The files for each official are in the Teacher's Book.

Tapescripts

Unit 1

Turnover Trouble

Dialogue 1

The Managing Director of Proteus (Manara) is explaining the situation to the new accountant.

Acc So you're a subsidiary of the Proteus Group which is based in Birmingham?

MD That's right. We're a public company and our shares are quoted on the London Stock Exchange.

Acc You must be doing well. I see the management accounts show a 20 per cent increase in turnover!

MD That's true but we also had a fall in our net profit.

Acc Oh, I see. Can you explain how that happened?

MD I'm not sure. You see, despite the recession our sales to Eastern Europe increased.

Acc So income from sales should have risen.

MD Yes, but we only increased sales by lowering the price of our main product. So our gross margin fell from 31 per cent to 14 per cent of sales.

Acc So your income from sales increased but your profits decreased!

MD I know. We hoped to make them rise by increasing sales of other products and maintaining our overall gross margin. But we had to absorb a price increase by one of our suppliers and this reduced our gross margin on our other products by 2 per cent. Now our net profit has fallen...

Dialogue 2

The Financial Controller of Proteus (Manara) Ltd phones the Managing Director.

FC I just wanted to say something about that financial report I gave you.

MD Yes, I think I see what's wrong. The export sales were good but not good enough.

FC That's right. Our overall sales total did not make enough to cover all our costs.

MD Yes, and I can see that the return on capital is now well below the minimum set by Head Office. How did that happen?

FC Well, it's because of the low profit, you see. And excess working capital. It's clear from the balance sheet.

MD Yes, I see. So what do you think we should do about it?

FC Well, we must report in detail on how much profit each product makes. This applies particularly to production costs; so we can see which products make a low gross profit and which products are doing well...

Dialogue 3 Listening for information

After reading the Financial Controller's memorandum, the Managing Director called him in for a more detailed discussion of the problem.

MD It still isn't clear to me why profits are down while sales are up. I know our overheads rose because I had to rent additional warehousing and take on more staff. But look at this $400,000 increase in sales! $300,000 came from the Protocap Energy Saver alone!

FC I think the answer's in your Profit and Loss statement. We've got to look at what has changed in it since the previous statement. We should try to understand how the increased fixed overhead costs and lower selling prices have affected the break-even point.

MD Yes, but I thought my increased sales would make up for the fall in budgeted gross margins.

FC Well, let's look at the figures in the Profit and Loss statement. You see, you have to calculate your break-even point, which is the point at which your income from sales covers all your costs.

MD I see. It's the point at which you make neither a loss nor a profit.

FC Exactly.

MD And how do you find it?

FC Well, there's a handy formula. What you do is you divide your operating expenses by your gross profit as a percentage of sales.

MD OK. So let's take the figures for the year before last. Our sales were $2,000,000 and our cost of sales $1,380,000 which made our gross profit $620,000. $620,000 as a percentage of $2,000,000 is thirty-one. Now our operating expenses for the same period were $520,000. So your formula is 520,000 divided by 31 over a hundred. Or 520,000,000 over 31.

FC Which makes $1,677,000.

MD So that's the break-even point for the year before last!

FC Which means you had to make $1,677,000 of gross profit to cover operating expenses.

Unit 2

A Question of Figures

Dialogue 1. Use of vocabulary

The Proteus Managing Director continues his discussion with the Financial Controller early in 1995.

FC Now in last year's figures, there was a 21 per cent increase in operating expenses. The worst increase was in the interest paid to the bank because of government stupidity in raising interest rates.

MD Then of course administration went up, but only by seven and a half per cent.

FC Yes these overheads wouldn't have been so bad but for the large inventory increases. These together with the steep rise in labour costs and factory overheads raised the total cost of sales by 27 per cent.

MD This meant our gross profit margin fell to only 27 per cent of sales. And the break even point rose to $2,333,000, an increase of 39 per cent over last year's figure.

FC In other words you would have needed an extra $656,000 of sales just to cover the increase in your operating expenses.

Listening for information

An accountant explains how to calculate return on capital. The financial information in the balance sheet is used by managers to tell the shareholders the return on their capital. This is the amount of profit expressed as a percentage of the capital invested in the company. The shareholders who provided the capital are interested in dividends which are paid out of the profits.

The capital of a company consists of fixed assets and current assets minus current liabilities.

We will use the balance sheet of Proteus (Manara) as an example. In 1993, the capital employed was M$780,000 and the net profit (see the Profit and Loss Account) was M$60,000. To calculate the return on the capital you work out what the net profit was as a percentage of the capital. So the calculation for 1993 is 60,000 over 780,000 times 100, which is 7.7 per cent.

But the net profit given at the end of the year was earned during the year, while the figure for the capital employed is what it was at the end of the year. So, to be more accurate, we should work out the average of capital employed for the year. This can be done for 1993 by taking figures on 31st December 1992 and 1993 and taking the average.

The capital employed on 31st December 1992 was M$660,000 and the amount for 31st December 1993 was M$780,000 and the average was therefore M$ 720,000. The calculation is 60,000 times 100 over 720,000, which is 600 over 72, which equals 8.3 per cent.

Dialogue 2. Use of vocabulary

The Proteus Managing Director continues his discussion with the Financial Controller, who advises him what to do about Proteus's falling profits.

MD OK. I understand what you're saying, but what do you think caused the fall in the gross margin? I thought that extra sales of the Protocap Energy Saver would produce even more profit. But the opposite has happened.

FC Yes, clearly the gross margin on the Protocap is too low. We must look at the figures in more detail – especially the costs.

MD That reminds me. Our borrowing costs – the bank manager rang me yesterday saying that he was worried about the increase in our overdraft. Why has our borrowing gone up so much since last year?

FC Well, mainly because we've been borrowing extra working capital and the costs of extra storage and personnel. Let's have a quick look at the 1993 Balance Sheet.

MD All right. But make it quick! I've got a meeting with a customer in ten minutes.

FC Well, this shouldn't take a minute. Our inventories were 40 per cent higher in 1994 than in 1993 and the customer receivables were up by 31 per cent. But note that sales rose by only 20 per cent. So we must control our working capital more effectively.
On the other hand we ended 1994 owing trade creditors 38 per cent more than in 1993, so the extra credit you got from them was financing most of the increase in the current assets. The rest, $90,000 was covered by the extra money we borrowed from our bank.

MD Yes, I see. But can you give me any suggestions for action now? I want to tell the managers as soon as possible.

FC Well, I suppose we could reduce sales of the Protocap Energy Saver, and try to increase the margins on all the other products. That would reduce our turnover, but it would certainly improve the profit situation.

MD Cut turnover! Is this some kind of joke? What do you think head office in Birmingham would say?

FC No, I'm quite serious. Just think about it. Our sales will fall but we'll be selling mostly products with higher gross margins. I know we won't be able to reduce some costs, particularly those which are fixed – they don't change with the sales volume, but overall we would end up with more dollars of profit. And our return on capital will certainly improve.

MD That's rather difficult to follow.

FC Is it?

MD Could you go over that again?

FC Certainly! It's easy to work out. If we could raise our gross margin to 33 per cent...

Unit 3

How Much Does It Cost?

Dialogue 1

It is July 1995. The Financial Controller is again discussing the financial position of the company with the Managing Director. The Production Manager is also present.

FC .... so overall the results of the first six months of 1995 are better than they were for the whole of 1994. Mind you, to make 2.2 per cent pre-tax profit on sales is a very poor performance and we are below the 1995 Plan.

MD Yes. That doesn't make it any better.

FC The latest forecast is that the net profit for the twelve months of 1995 will be below our Plan, better than the 1994 figure, but not much above the figure for 1993. One good sign for the second six months is that both inventories and financial costs are down.

MD So what are the main problem areas?

FC Well, the main one is the low margin on sales of the Energy Saver, which is depressing profits. I must say that from a purely financial point of view, unless we can improve its sales and profit contribution, it would be better to consider discontinuing this product.

MD Well, you know what the answer is to that: it's the Proteus Group's policy to increase worldwide sales of the Energy Saver, so there's no question of dropping it.

FC Well, I feel...

MD As a matter of fact I've got a copy of the latest Head Office directive dealing with the Protocap. You can read it in your own office. You'll see that our main task is to boost sales volumes and values of the Protocap and reduce unit costs.
On the other hand, I have already discussed the problem of increasing total sales value with the Marketing Manager . It's clear we can't raise prices because our competitors' prices are already 2 per cent below our price in most markets.

FC So our problem is how to boost sales and cut costs. Any problems in the production area?

Dialogue 2

The Managing Director has just been talking about the directive from Head Office which says Proteus(Manara) should concentrate on the Protocap. The Financial Controller asks the Production Manager about his problems and they discuss various practical ways of carrying out the company policy of promoting the Protocap.

FC – .... how to boost sales and cut costs. Any problems in the production area?

PM Yes, quite serious ones, caused by short production runs on the Protocap. A lot of time is spent setting up each run. Also the planning and administration for each run is very time-consuming and expensive.

MD Yes I am aware of that, but there's little that we can do in the short term except go for higher sales volumes. What are the financial effects of doing this?

FC The unit costs of production are 20 per cent above plan. This is because production runs have to be charged with labour and overheads on the basis of total time spent in the factory. This includes the setting-up – and so we are always exceeding our cost targets per unit.

PM One way to reduce costs is to use other materials for the Protocap. I could also reorganise the assembly lines to increase the production rate. But to get significant economies we'd need to double the number we produce.

MD That's a tall order. However, Head Office engineering staff have already made some suggestions for technical improvements. Yes. They are coming over here from the UK next week to discuss them. What I really want to do is to reduce the cost of the Energy Saver, hold its selling price or even reduce it by 5 per cent. We could invest say $50,000 in an aggressive advertising campaign and offer customers quantity discounts.

Dialogue 3

The Managing Director, the Production Manager and the Financial Controller have just been talking about ways of reducing the production costs and boosting the volume of sales of the Protocap. The Managing Director now tells the others how he wants them organised so that they can deal with the task in hand.

MD We must see what extra turnover we need to achieve our net profit target, and then decide how to get those extra sales.

FC I'll need a sales forecast by product and by market with expected selling prices and selling costs.

MD I'll get together with the Marketing Manager and produce the figures you need. It'll take a day or two. Meanwhile I want the two of you to produce a plan for cost reductions on the Energy Saver and show me the possible effects on the company's net profits. Gentlemen, the principle task is to boost the Protocap sales, and we'll achieve that by concentrating on our overseas markets. So we must find the most effective way of strengthening our position in Central and Eastern Europe.
I'm setting up a task force to map out a strategy for expansion. It will consist of you two and the Marketing Manager. I'll draft some terms of reference for you tomorrow and let Head Office know of our intentions.

Unit 4

Doubtful Ratios

Listening 1. Return on Capital

The Managing Director of Proteus (Manara) has to attend a meeting at Head Office and explain his poor financial figures to the Group Chairman. So he needs to understand not only the ratios used by his accountants, but also the adverse ratios in the balance sheet.

MD By the way, next week I've got the Group Meeting in Birmingham, so perhaps you could go over the adverse ratios to make sure I'm clear on what they mean!

FC OK, let's begin with the key ratio – our return on capital. Although it only summarises our profitability, this ratio and the earnings per share are the ones which most interest the shareholders and affect the Group dividend.

MD If I understand it correctly, we take profit as a percentage of capital employed...

FC Yes, but don't forget, it's profit after tax, and we usually express profit in relation to the average net capital employed during the year. That's because our profit is earned throughout the year.

MD By 'net', you mean after deducting all liabilities?

FC That's right.

MD So if our profit in 1994 was M$12,000 and our

average capital employed was about M$776,000, our return on capital was, let's see, 1.5 percent!! That can't be right. It's ridiculously low! Interest rates last year average 8-9 per cent. Then there's inflation. And wasn't our return on capital in 1990 about 12 or 13 per cent?

FC Yes, that's true. But to be fair, a low return on capital was foreseen in the 1994 Financial Plan, because of our heavy investment in the Protocap Energy Saver.

MD Yes, but not 1.5 per cent! Which is why, for us, it's a case of expand or bust! We should have been properly financed when we were established here in Manara. The Group have always preferred us to obtain our own finance once they'd invested their $500,000 of share capital.

FC We did ask for additional support, but at the time they said the exchange risk was too great and they preferred us to borrow in Manara dollars even if local interest rates were higher than in the UK. They accepted a lower return on capital.

Unit 4

TWO Listening 2. Customer receivables

The Financial Controller and the Managing Director continue their conversation. Listen carefully for the phrases used by the speakers to connect their speech. These phrases connect with what has gone before and lead in to what they are going to say.

MD All right, now let's look at the customer receivables. How can I explain those to the Chairman?

FC Group procedures express receivables as days of sales to make them comparable with other companies of the Group.
Now, if in December 1994 our receivables were $550 thousand and our sales for the year were $2.4 million, and if we assume there are 240 working days in a year (as the procedure requires) the average sales were $10,000 per day.

MD I see. So that means $550 thousand worth of receivables divided by one day of sales or $10 thousand, gives an average of 55. That's days of sales. So if our normal credit terms are 30 days, these people are getting 25 days free finance from us! What was the ratio for 1993?

FC Let's see – sales of 2 million – that's $8,333 per day and receivables were $420 thousand which divided $8,333, gives us 50.4 days.

MD Even that wasn't a satisfactory ratio. What's the average for the group?

FC It's difficult to make comparisons of this kind between different countries but I believe that 40-45 days would be considered acceptable.

MD Well, we're still ten days too high. You're responsible for the credit control, so I'd be glad if you could let me have an action plan to get this figure down to 45 days by the end of the year. Now let's look at inventories...

Unit 5

The Way Forward
ONE Dialogue 1

The Financial Controller is talking with his subordinate, the Financial Accountant. They are discussing changes which must be made to make the Proteus accounting system conform fully with group accounting procedures. They also have to ensure that the system produces the information needed to develop an improved cost accounting system based on activity costing.

FC I see that the General Accounting System has been running on the minicomputer for nine months. So you and your staff should be familiar with each module.

FA Yes, it was difficult at the beginning, and we had to use the telephone helpline a lot and we did find a few bugs. But on the whole we got good software support.

FC Well, I hope those bugs have all been ironed out because now we've got to make some changes to the whole system...

FA Changes now? Isn't it rather late in the day for changes? Our financial year ends in only four months.

FC I think it'll be OK. the software itself won't have to be modified. But we must make greater use of the General Ledger and Costing modules so as to produce the additional information which the Group Finance Department needs and to develop an activity-based costing system. Later next year, we shall probably have to install another company on the system.

FA Will that be a wholly-owned subsidiary or an associated company?

FC It could be either. In any case, we must be ready to use the system to produce consolidated accounts.

TWO Dialogue 2

The Financial Controller continues his conversation with the Financial Accountant. They go on to talk about things they will have to do as a result of making changes in the Proteus accounting system.

FC In any case, we must be ready to use the system to produce consolidated accounts.

FA That means we'll have to modify the whole coding system. It'll affect the Nominal Ledger Codes, the Cost Centre Codes, even the Departmental Codes...

FC That's certainly true. But don't forget we must still be able to produce our local Manaran Statutory Accounts in the exact format laid down by the Accounting Law. So we can't change the Chart of Accounts too much.

FA It shouldn't be a problem. The software allows us to use two sets of accounting codes. We could use one set for UK reporting purposes and the other for Manaran Statutory Accounts. We can also add more digits to the Nominal Ledger Code to allow us to analyse the transactions by activity.

FC Excellent! Now let's see. For each activity we'll have

to calculate the investment of fixed assets as well as the revenue and expenses which it generates.

FA It's going to take a lot of work to calculate expenses by activity such as depreciation, energy consumption, maintenance, the cost of space used, insurance and so on.

FC Yes, you're right there. The problem is to decide which activities we must use. We definitely need to track expenses in the areas of procurement, materials handling, inspection, production, order processing, selling and after-sales service...

FA The list is endless. I'd better talk to the departmental managers and agree with them the key activities in their areas. Mind you, we could end up with too many activities...

Unit 6

Evaluating a Project

ONE Listening 1. A potential liability

The Financial Controller of Proteus (Manara) is on the 'phone to the Manager of the Treasury Department of the parent company in Birmingham.

FC Look, I really need to discuss our local currency borrowings. As you must have read from my report, we're having a difficult time this year and our borrowings have soared.

MTD Yes, that was quite a jump, wasn't it!

FC The latest problem is that our bankers here won't lend any more money on the strength of our 1994 financial statements. They want security. They're asking for either collateral or a parent company guarantee.

MTD Well, what collateral have you got?

FC Unfortunately, since we rent our factory, we could only offer machinery and vehicles. I suspect they'd only be interested in the vehicles. Our machinery is too specialised and wouldn't realise much on a crash sale. And the vehicles are mainly customised trucks.

MTD Well, as you know, the Group Directors are extremely reluctant to give guarantees, especially to overseas operations and more so where the potential liability is in a currency subject to fluctuations. Do you think they would accept a Letter of Comfort?

FC No, I've already asked them. They prefer a guarantee in Manara dollars.

MTD Well, at present the group policy is to keep contingent liabilities to a minimum, ever since the Accounting Standard has required them to be reported in the UK statutory accounts.

Two. Listening 2

FC Well, I must get back to our bankers with a concrete proposal within the next ten days. What do you suggest?

MTD I'll talk to the Group Financial Director. Logically we have only three options – one is a parent company guarantee or a cross guarantee from another European subsidiary with assets free, as collateral – and that's complicated enough! Failing that, we could raise either a direct sterling or Eurodollar loan. Lastly, we could make a direct investment in Proteus (Manara).

FCM Obviously, the last would be preferable, especially since we are planning this major expansion in Central and Eastern Europe.

MTD I agree. But that depends on whether the Main Board approves your expansion project. Look, we ought to try to persuade your bankers not to insist on a guarantee, at least until a decision is reached on the Manara project.

FCM Yes, I agree entirely. It does occur to me that, if the Group Financial Director could come to Manara and have a meeting with our bankers, he might convince them that Birmingham might support you. Or could he not invite them to Birmingham to see the main Proteus factory? Then they might accept a Letter of Comfort or postpone the deadline for a guarantee.

MTD It's certainly worth a try. Let me talk to the chief and I'll fax you an answer within 48 hours...

Unit 7

Reviewing the Financial Base

Listening 1. Explaining and comparing

Listen for the phrases used to explain the audit situation of the Manaran subsidiary of Proteus and the expressions used to compare it with UK auditing practice.

Auditor I've brought an English translation of my Audit Report. The official version is in Manaran and has to be submitted to the Ministry of Finance at Manara City within the next 10 days. But before submitting it, I want to discuss its contents with both of you.

MD Thank you. But I'm not too clear if this report is of any use to our Head Office in Birmingham.

Auditor As soon as I was appointed, I met the Financial Controller and explained to him what work has to be done for a Manaran audit. We both agreed that our auditing requirements here differ from those of the UK and I believe he passed on the information to your Head Office.

FC Yes, I did. Actually Manaran auditing requirements requirements are fairly close to the UK auditing standards but there are some differences, which means that a second audit usually has to be performed by Manaran auditors appointed directly by Proteus.

MD (to FC) So we have to pay for two audits!

FC The Manaran audit is cheaper because it focuses mainly on the financial statements and records. The audit for the Proteus Group, on the other hand, involves extensive testing and review of our financial systems and controls. The other problem is that the layout and content of

Manaran statutory accounts is different from the accounts we submit to Head Office.

Auditor I can tell you one thing. The Manaran Audit report is used by our Ministry of Finance to decide whether or not to renew your company's trading licence for the next year. So it is important.

MD (hastily) Oh, I see. So what will you say in your report?

Auditor My report shows a satisfactory position and my task was made easier thanks to the help of your accounting staff. Here's a copy for your to keep.

MD Well, that's a relief. Have you got any other comments to make?

Unit 8

Obtaining Finance

Listening 1. Discussion of Treasury Management and Foreign Exchange

The Managing Director of Proteus Manara, the Financial Controller and the Treasury Manager from Birmingham discuss treasury management and foreign exchange.

MD .....I've decided to sit in on your discussion because I need to understand how we should manage and report on our foreign currency borrowings.

TM Well, the present situation is that Birmingham wants you to finance your expansion through borrowing in Manara dollars.

FC I take it that means using part of these borrowings to finance our proposed investment in the East?

TM Actually the Board has not yet made a decision, but you must consider borrowing either in Manara dollars or in the currency of a selected Eastern country, if that's at all possible ...

MD But surely the Board has already decided where we are to be funded?

TM Not entirely. Between us, some Board members are undecided about the Group's long-term financing strategy. They fear that heavy additional borrowing will increase the Group's gearing. UK investors may become alarmed and sell their shares, and this would force the share price down.

FC (to MD) You see, if we invest in Manara and Eastern Europe, the assets acquired will be in the local currency and may be exposed to exchange losses if sterling strengthens. So it makes sense to take out Manara dollar loans to finance these assets in order to hedge or minimise possible losses. Or, better still, to borrow in the country where we want to set up.

MD You mean that losses from translating local currency assets into sterling will be covered in the consolidated balance sheet by the gains when translating local currency borrowings ...

FC ... and vice versa ...

TM Suppose we acquire fixed capital assets in Manara for M$200,000, then at today's exchange rate of $20 to the Pound the assets will be reported to Head Office at a value of £10,000.

MD Yes ...

TM If by December 31st, when our financial year ends, the exchange rate is M$25 to the pound because sterling has strengthened against the Manara dollar, the assets will reported at £8,000.

MD A difference of £2,000 – a loss, I presume.

FC Yes, so if we borrow $200,000 to finance the purchase of assets, a loan initially translated as £10,000 becomes a loan of only £8,000 at the end of the year.

MD Fine, I get it. A loss of £2,000 from translating the assets is offset by the gain of £2,000 when translating the loan.

FC That's why we need to persuade our Manaran Bank to lend us in dollars ... and without giving them a Proteus Group guarantee.

MD Or an Eastern bank to lend to us in their currency.

FC That, too, seems a likely possibility.

Unit 9

The Path to Partnership

ONE Dialogue 1. Taxation and Dividends

At the Proteus office in Manara City the Financial Controller, a Barakonian accountant and the Accounts Manager from Proteus's Birmingham office discuss taxation and dividends in Manara and Barakonia

FC How are things in Barakonia? Is what I've heard true, that the liberalisation process is extending to the tax system?

BA Regrettably not, I'm afraid. The government is keeping an iron grip on the economy by a heavy burden of taxation on individuals and companies. But indirect taxes, such as sales tax and VAT have been avoided.

AM I know what you mean. The Chancellor, in his Autumn Budget has just increased taxation all round.

FC Well, in Manara we seem to have the best of all worlds. We have lower taxes than either Barakonia or the UK. Also it's simpler to remit dividends to foreign investors. But it's not all a bed of roses. VAT is going up and there are going to be special duties on luxury goods, petrol and tobacco.

BA What about corporation tax?

FC The standard rate is coming down from 40 per cent to 35 per cent but the first 100 thousand Manara dollars of profit are taxed at 25 per cent and there's an allowance for training.

AM Yes, I think the authorities here are going in the right direction. But what interests us most at the moment is how repatriated dividends are treated.

BA Well in Barakonia no dividends are remittable to foreign shareholders for the first three years of an investment. Thereafter dividends are restricted to 10 per cent per year and are subject to a withholding tax of 5 per cent.

FC In Manara it's 10 per cent from the outset. But companies which withdraw invested capital within five years of when it was invested suffer a penalty tax of 5 per cent of the total remitted. ...Ah, here's the coffee and some Schplugotonic water from Barakonia...

TWO Dialogue 2. Taxation and dividends

The Financial Controller, the Barakonian accountant and the Accounts Manager from the Birmingham office continue their conversation.

BA Hmm. You've got a good brand of Schplugotonic, I see. As I was saying, the taxation situation in Barakonia is not very encouraging to foreign investors.

FC Oh dear. What about social security

BA Yes, I was coming to that. You see the government has to featherbed all the Barakonians who are not accustomed to unemployment by ensuring good unemployment benefits and ensuring that all employers pay their social insurance.

AM I suppose that leads to firms employing as few people as possible and making as much of the workforce as possible redundant.

BA That's right. And not all business expenses are tax-deductible. For example, allowances on fixed capital assets allows plant to be depreciated on a straight line basis. There are no exceptions, and any additional depreciation charges are not allowable as necessary business expenses.

FC What about remitting dividends on investments?

BA As I mentioned before, you can't remit anything for three years from the date of investment. You have to take a long-term view.

AM So, what you're saying is, if we put money into Barakonia it has to be a long-term investment and we won't expect to see any return in the first five years.

BA Yes, that's quite right.

FC So it's not surprising Birmingham won't help us, and we will have to finance any Barakonian venture out of after-tax profits from Manara. There will be no dividends to pay to Birmingham and so no withholding tax. Another advantage for us is that Manaran tax law allows us to depreciate fixed assets on a reducing balance over ten years.

Unit 10

Deciding on Partners

The Proteus Financial Controller, Production Manager and Marketing Manager discuss the costing of the Protocap Energy Saver.

FC If you look at the detailed cost and profit projection for the Energy Saver you can see that the unit cost of materials does not fall when sales increase towards the end of 1996.

PM Yes, that's amazing. Even if my planned reorganisation of production methods reduces total labour time on the Energy Saver from 5.6 to 4.5 hours by 1996, the unit manufacturing cost as a percentage of sales will remain around 63 per cent. So what's happening and what can we do?

FC Well, at present we have to buy all the main sub-assemblies from our factory in Birmingham – that's Group policy. It also helps to repatriate profit to the UK through inflating the inter-company transfer price. We also have to pay the freight costs which add about 10 per cent to the imported price.

MM We also have to absorb any exchange fluctuations.

PM Yes. But we can cut costs by finding local suppliers for as many sub-assemblies as possible.

MM That's fine. But how can we be sure of the quality and reliability of locally-produced assemblies?

PM That's my job. It'll be tricky but there's no point in ignoring local sourcing wherever possible. Otherwise we'll lose one of the main advantages of producing in Barakonia. Another one is the faster production rate over there. What was it?

FC It'll take the Barakonia plant, once it's going, 50 minutes less than the factory in Manara to make the Energy Saver. That'll bring down the direct labour costs and the allocation of factory overheads even after we have revised our present allocation methods – I mean, to take in the cost of activities in the logistics and production processes.

MM All this should enable me to set a more competitive price.

FC That should bring in a substantial increase in sales which will in turn reduce unit costs. Our indirect and fixed overheads will be spread over a greater number of units of production.

Answer Key

Unit 1

Page 6

B Discussion 1: Before Reading

For explanation of terms, see the Glossary on pages 172-185

D Vocabulary

1 a)	(i)	d)	(iv)
b)	(iii)	e)	(i) and (iii)
c)	(i)	f)	(iii)

2
- a) group
- b) based in
- c) public limited company
- d) the Stock Exchange
- e) Managing Director
- f) management accounts
- g) recession
- h) suppliers
- i) paid

Page 8

E Listening

See tapescript.

F Grammar

1 *...based in Birmingham*
- a) The Protocap has components supplied by sub-contractors.
- b) They make electric cars equipped with battery chargers.
- c) The accountant showed us the half-yearly results prepared for the board meeting.
- d) They were drinking wine imported from Hungary.

Page 9
- e) He was worried by the fall in net profit caused by the reduced margin of their main products.
- f) In the financial plan submitted to the head office in Birmingham, he decided to increase the sales of their secondary products.
- g) The Protocap made by Proteus' subsidiary company was cheaper to produce in Manara than in Birmingham.

3 **whose**
- a) There are hundreds of accountants whose addresses can be found in the 'phone book.
- b) It's a large engineering company whose factories make components for car manufacturers.
- c) They are exporters of foodstuffs whose supermarkets are all over the country.
- d) He bought shares in BM Engineering whose value fell soon after he bought them.
- e) There were hundreds of passengers in the departure lounge whose flights had been delayed by the fog.
- f) They were worried about the company whose production costs had risen sharply.
- g) Production was delayed at the factory whose main building had been damaged by fire.
- h) The government whose economic policies had failed lowered interest rates.
- i) The manager wanted to know why the company whose turnover had increased was making less profit.
- j) The Financial Controller whose advice had been asked said that prices must be raised.

4 *Despite*
- a) turnover
- b) healthy sales

Page 10
- c) costs
- d) smaller margins
- e) his lowering his price

5 *Transitive and intransitive verbs*
- a) fallen/decreased
- b) lowered/reduced
- c) risen/increased/gone up
- d) raise/increase

6
- a) reduced/lowered
- b) risen/increased
- c) showed....rise/increase
- d) showed....fall/decrease

Page 11
- e) fall/decrease
- f) had fallen/decreased
- g) reduce/lower
- h) raise/increase,
- i) raising/increasing
- j) go up .... decreases/falls/drops

G Discussion II: *Comprehension*

Proteus makes electrical and public lighting equipment.
It also makes an energy saver – the Protocap.
It's based in Birmingham.
It makes electrical equipment, for street lighting, public buildings and sports stadiums.
Net profits fell although turnover had increased.
A public limited company issues shares which can be traded on the market. The shareholders are liable for the

company's losses only to the extent of their shares (the money they have put into the company).
The Managing Director is the chief executive of a company, who is a shareholder and is responsible for the day-to-day running of the company.
The London Stock Exchange is the most important UK market for company shares and government stocks.
The profit of a business after deduction of expenses.
The gross margin: the difference between the selling price and the manufacturing cost.
Turnover is the total value of sales during a year.
Management accounts: financial information prepared for managers on sales, costs, credit and profitability.

Page 12
I Vocabulary
1 a) extract from a memorandum
b) the strong export sales
c) we have not generated enough gross profit
d) operating and financial expenses
e) return on capital
f) This arises from
g) excess working capital
h) reporting on
i) product profitability
j) is essential ...... to identify

2 a) improved e) identify
b) increased f) identify, pinpoint
c) cover g) generate
d) absorb h) set

3 (1) Controller (8) set
(2) Director (9) low
(3) strong (10) the
(4) months (11) on
(5) the (12) production
(6) operating (13) products
(7) capital

Page 13
J Use of Vocabulary: *Dialogue 2*
For dialogue completion, see the tapescripts.

K Listening for information
1 .... why profits were down and sales were up
2 Warehousing and labour (he had to take on more staff).
3 M$400,000
4 The Profit and Loss Statement

Page 14
5 fixed overhead costs
6 The break-even point
7 It's the point at which income from sales covers all costs.
8 M$2,000,000
9 M$620,000
10 M$520,000
11 M$1,677,000
12 The break-even point gives you the figure your gross profit must be to cover operating expenses.

L Problem-solving
1 The break-even point
For 1993 it was 520 divided by 31 = M$1,677,000
For 1994 it was 630 divided by 27 = M$2,333,333

2 Diagram completion

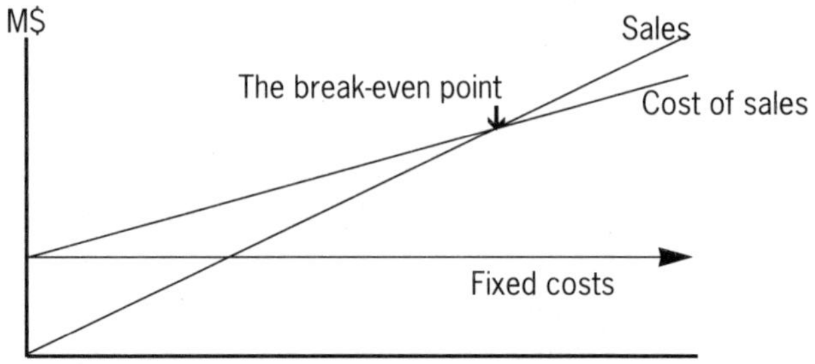

3 Because the break-even point for that year is M$2,333,333 or M$656,000 more than in 1993. In other words, they have to make M$656,000 more of sales to cover additional operating costs.

Page 15
N Listening and note-taking
Increased *exports/sales* to Central and Eastern Europe
Fall in Profits; increased warehousing and *labour* costs
Increase in amount of interest paid to bank
Expenses/Overheads have increased faster than income.
Smaller *fixed overhead costs*
Reduce the *break-even point*
Increase *the selling price*

Unit 2

Page 17
B Discussion I
1 For 'period', see *Accounting Period* in the Glossary.
2 A Balance Sheet is like a photograph of the financial condition of a company on one day.

Page 18
D Vocabulary
2 d) 3 g) 4 d)

Page 19
E Grammar: Language for Calculation
2 The net profit as a percentage of sales in 1994 in figures and in words:
a) $\frac{12 \times 100}{2400} = 0.5\%$
b) Twelve over two thousand four hundred times a hundred, *or* Twelve times a hundred over two thousand four hundred equals/point five per cent/nought point five per cent.

3 Purchases went up by M$380,000 to M$1,480,000 in 1994. The opening inventory went up by M$20,000 to M$250,000 in 1994. Interest costs rose by M$10,000 to M$30,000 in 1994. Labour costs increased by M$ 55,000 to M$245,000 in 1994.

Page 20

4 a) There was an increase in overheads
b) There are several subsidiaries of Proteus in other countries. *or*
There are several Proteus subsidiaries in other countries.
c) There was an actual fall in net profits.
d) There was a rise in sales to Central and Eastern Europe.
e) There was a gross margin of 31 per cent on the Protocap.
f) Now there is a margin of only 14 per cent.
g) There was an increase in prices by one of the suppliers.
h) There is another problem.
i) There will be a saving in production costs.
j) There will be a fall of 37 per cent in sales.

F Listening I
See tapescript

Page 21
H Vocabulary and dictionary work
Fixed assets: c) Debtors: f) Creditors: g)

Page 22
Shareholder's equity: i) (j) may be only part of the equity.)

2 a)	Fixed assets:	factory buildings, lorries, machinery
	Current assets:	money in the bank, unpaid invoices, unsold stock, raw materials
b)	Payables:	electricity bill, telephone bill
	Receivables:	Unsettled customer accounts, trade credits received
	Inventories:	Unsold goods, spare parts for machines, unfinished parts

3 *Definitions*

a) inventories	h) overhead
b) turnover	i) payables
c) overdraft	j) liabilities
d) asset	k) capital (employed)
e) receivables	l) subsidiary
f) Balance Sheet	m) margin
g) profits	n) account

Page 23
I Phrase building
(The oblique signs / indicate an alternatives)
Adjective-noun phrases

1 The following combinations are possible:
A(The/My/Another/Our/Your) (large/substantial/healthy) (gross/net) profit; (large/substantial) bank overdraft; (A/The/Our/Your) (large/substantial) gross margin; (large/substantial) opening stock; (large/substantial) production overheads; (large/substantial) overseas (net/fixed/current) assets; (overseas/current/company) (debtors/creditors); (large/substantial/valuable) overseas (net/current) liabilities; (substantial) (net/fixed) overseas capital; (large/substantial/healthy) (annual/company) turnover; (large/valuable) (overseas) (sales) subsidiary; (large/substantial/valuable) (production/sales); (large/substantial/valuable/healthy) profit increase; (company/current) bank account; healthy (company/annual) Balance Sheet

2 *Verb-adjective-noun phrases*
The following verbs:
increase, have, reduce, calculate, raise
may all be used with:
margin, overheads, stock, debtors, creditors, liabilities, turnover and overdraft
The following combinations are also possible:
increase, have, reduce, accumulate, purchase assets

increase, have, reduce, accumulate, raise	capital
accumulate, purchase	stock
accumulate	liabilities
increase, make, reduce, calculate, raise	profit
have, make, purchase	a subsidiary
have, calculate, reduce, lower	an increase
have, reduce	an account
have	Balance Sheet

Page 24
J Grammar

a) You could work out/calculate your gross profit by multiplying units sold by the gross margin.
b) You could work out/calculate your overheads by deducting production costs from total costs (of sales).
c) You could work out/calculate the net profit by subtracting tax from gross profit.
d) You could work out/calculate current assets by adding stock to debtors.
e) You can work out/calculate current liabilities by adding short-term loans to taxes and payables.
f) You could work out/calculate net assets by deducting total liabilities from total assets.
g) You could work out/calculate total liabilities by adding current liabilities to long-term loans and debts.

K Listening and Information

1 One purpose of the Balance Sheet is to show shareholders the return on their capital.
2 It's the amount of profit as a percentage of capital invested.
3 They're interested in the return on capital because it will be used to determine their dividends.
4 It's the fixed assets plus current assets minus current liabilities.
5 The return on capital for 1993 - 1994 should be calculated as follows:
$$\frac{\text{The net profit of 1994} \times 100}{\text{The average capital employed}}$$
$$= \frac{12 \times 100}{\text{The average capital employed}} = \frac{1200}{780 + 792 \text{ divided by } 2}$$
$$= \frac{1200}{786} = 1.53\%$$

L Listening II
See tapescript.

Page 26
M Vocabulary
borrowing costs – interest
overdraft – money owed to the bank on the current account
working capital – money used to pay business expenses
storage – warehousing
personnel – labour
trade creditors – unpaid suppliers
covered – paid for
sales volume – the number of items sold

2 *Collocations*
borrowing costs, extra storage, extra personnel, customer receivables, working capital

N Grammar
1 *Showing understanding and agreement*
a) I see what you mean.
b) I know how you feel.
c) I see what you're driving at.
d) I appreciate what you say/you're saying

Page 27
2 *Indirect thought or speech about doubtful events*
a) If we cut .... would say?
b) He hoped .... would pay for ....
c) The FC explained it would be necessary to ....
d) The MD said he would understand better if the FC explained ....
e) The MD hoped the accountant would provide the answers.

3 *Indirect thought or speech about prior events*
a) .... though there had been ....
b) .... explained gross margins had become ....
c) .... realised something had gone wrong.
d) .... thought not everything had been understood.
e) .... said .... had arrived.

4 a) .... told .... was ....
b) .... said .... wanted ....
c) .... realised .... was ....
d) .... understood .... lay ....
e) .... became .... had to go ....

Page 28
5 a) .... thinks .... will be ....
b) .... says .... will come ....
c) .... hope I will see ....

6 a) There has been ....
b) We have taken on ....
c) .... have risen.
d) .... has made a report ....
e) .... has become necessary to ....

7 a) He's been drinking beer all night long.
b) He's been talking ....
c) .... has been rising ....
d) .... has been growing ....
e) .... has been continuing

Page 29
8 *Qualifying the verb*
a) The costs should be examined with greater care.
b) It doesn't pay to do things in such a hurry.
c) The calculation could be done more accurately.
d) So we must control our working capital more effectively.
e) The accountant explained everything again more clearly.

Unit 3

Page 32
C Vocabulary
1 a) Group Export Manager
b) the Group Main Board
c) supplier of public lighting systems
d) the flagship product in the Proteus range
e) strategically important
f) associated companies
g) give top priority
h) formulating strategies to achieve these aims
i) implementing plans
j) successful penetration of the market
k) establishing a permanent presence
l) The following options should be considered ...
m) a substantial increase in the advertising budget
n) joint venture
o) exclusive distributor
p) dedicated distributor
q) borrowings
r) reluctant
s) It is a matter of the utmost urgency ...
t) Solutions to these problems should be found with a view to pursuing the group objectives outlined above

2 a) long-term aim
b) establish
c) suppliers
d) achieve these aims
e) with a view to
f) implement
g) penetrated (established a foothold)
h) substantial

Page 33
i) appointed
j) solution to

3 The following combinations are possible:
long-term, worldwide, marketing, advertising, joint *venture*
long-term, worldwide, marketing, advertising, group *objectives*

exclusive, marketing, substantial, advertising, group *budget*
long-term, market, substantial, advertising *increase*
exclusive, product *range*
long-term, market *penetration*
associated, dedicated, long-term world-wide *supplier*
long-term, worldwide, marketing, advertising, joint *aim*
associated, marketing, advertising *company*
associated, exclusive, dedicated, world-wide *distributor*
long-term, worldwide, marketing, advertising, *strategies*

4 *Synonyms*

borrowing – overdraft	strategy – plan of action
option – choice	implement – carry out
aims – objectives	consider – think about
permanent – long term	substantial – big
establish – set up	exclusive – sole
formulate – design	outline – describe

Page 34

D Grammar

1 a) Sales should be increased by 30 per cent.
b) You should become the largest suppliers of paint in the North.
c) You should plan to export to China.
d) Herbals should aim to borrow up to $6,000,000 for expansion.

2 *Impersonal passive*

It has been decided that a distributor should be appointed in Zambia.
It has been decided that sales should be increased in Barakonia.
It has been decided that sales should be reduced.
It has been decided that it should be reduced.
It has been decided that it should become a long term aim to ....
It has been decided that it should be established as a world-wide supplier of ....
It has been decided that Proteus should be established as a world-wide supplier of ....
It has been decided that costs should be reduced.

3 a) They decided that the Protocap should become the main ....
b) They decided that subsidiary and associated companies should give top ....
c) They decided that the Protocap Energy Saver should become a ....
d) They decided that the plans should be implemented ....
e) It has been decided that each company in the Group should establish itself ....
f) It has been decided Proteus Manara should establish a permanent ....
g) It has been decided that the following options should be considered:

Page 35

h) It is a matter of the utmost urgency that solutions to the problem (of ....) should be found.
i) It is extremely important that one should understand the financial health of a company before investing in it.

4 a) of b) in c) up d) to e) in

5 a) A carefully calculated forecast
b) A thoughtfully formulated strategy
c) A strongly implemented plan
d) A strongly supported policy
e) A permanently established presence

E Discussion

(Answers are in the same order as the questions.)
It was from the Group Export Manager in Birmingham.
The Managing Director of Proteus, Manara
On 30th June 1995
It was about export policy for the Protocap.
It said Proteus should become a world-wide supplier of public lighting systems.
It said the Protocap was a strategically important product.
It stated the importance of the Protocap saying it should become the flagship product of the Group.
It said associated companies and subsidiaries should give priority to it.
It said subsidiaries should formulate strategies in line with the stated policy of the Group.
It expected formulated aims to be achieved by early 1997.
Each company in the Group should establish itself permanently in the market it was responsible for.
Proteus Manara should continue its successful penetration of the market in Central and Eastern Europe.
It should establish a permanent presence there.
It should consider various ways of doing this.
The options were to increase advertising, set up subsidiaries, set up joint ventures and/or to appoint exclusive or dedicated distributors.
The main problem was finance. Borrowings were already high. Banks in Manara were already reluctant to lend more.
To find solutions to the problems so Group objectives could be pursued.

Page 37

G Vocabulary

1 a) prediction
b) price reduction
c) payment

Page 38

H Listening I

See tapescript.

Page 39

I Vocabulary

1 *Further practice*

a) results	g) discontinuing
b) performance	h) dropping
c) forecast	i) directives
d) depressing	j) dealing with

e) improve
f) contributions
k) boosted
l) reduce

2 *Compound nouns*

financial	contribution
problem	areas
profit	areas, contribution
worldwide	sales, sales value
head office	directive, costs
unit	costs
total	sales, costs, sales value, contribution

J Grammar

1 *Sentence connectors*

So overall	Therefore, in general,
Mind you	But you have to be careful
As a matter of fact	Actually, I
On the other hand	But against that is
So our problem is	Therefore, what we have to do is

Page 40

3 *Commenting*
a) But to borrow money when interest rates are high is expensive.
b) But to run up too big an inventory is unwise.
c) But to have a profitable flagship product is advantageous.

4 *Indirect speech*
a) The Financial Controller said that the overall results in January – June 1995 were better than 1994.
b) The Financial Controller said that it would be better to discontinue making this product.
c) The Financial Controller said that Proteus would have to reduce turnover.

Page 41

6 a) So there's no question of selling the Lodz factory.
b) So there's no question of opening the exhibition before the Queen arrives.
c) So there's no question of returning to the bad old days.

7 a) Have you seen the Balance Sheet showing the latest position?
b) Which are the operating costs causing the most problems?
c) I'll show you some figures proving my point.
d) There are several problems needing to be dealt with.

K Listening II

a) production run
b) time-consuming
c) unit cost
d) setting-up time
e) cost targets per unit
f) reorganise the assembly lines
g) production rate
h) to get significant economies
i) a tall order
j) invest
k) an aggressive advertising campaign
l) quantity discounts

Page 42

1 **Listening III**
a) to achieve our net profit target
b) a sales forecast by product and by market
c) concentrating on
d) the most cost effective way
e) task force
f) come up with a strategy for expansion
g) terms of reference

Unit 4

Page 46

C Vocabulary

1 a) ratios b) forecasts c) material costs
d) consumption e) accounting ratios
f) balance sheet ratios g) inventory
h) factory overheads
i) selling and administrative expenses j) receivables

2 a) concerned at b) reported c) slightly up on
d) gross profit e) below Plan f) a reduction in selling price or sales discounting g) For the year to date
h) in line with Plan j) inventory

3 a) concerned at b) proceed c) requires d) analysis
e) indicate f) steps will be taken g) intend
h) current inventory

Page 47

D Grammar

2 a) Raw materials should be reduced to 42 per cent of sales.
b) These ratios should follow the Plan.
c) The average should be reduced to 32 days.
d) Factory overheads should be brought down to 4 per cent of sales.

3 a) It is vital to produce a product development plan before visiting Warsaw.
b) It is of the utmost importance to examine the balance sheet ratios as soon as possible.
c) It is important to put the finances of Proteus Manara on a firm basis before expanding overseas.
d) It is essential to look at the costing system first of all.
e) It would be useful for the Managing Director to go over the finances carefully with the Financial Controller before coming to Birmingham.
f) It is crucial for the Production Manager to work out a plan to reduce inventory levels.

Page 48

5 *Determiners*
a) One among others, no particular one in mind
b) There is only one flagship product.
c) There's only one world.
d) One among several possible plans
e) sales, in general

f) no particular three weeks
g) There's only one bit of time that can be concurrent
h) Many among a large number
i) competition in general
j) one increase but no particular one
k) short production runs in general, not a particular one
l) same as k)

Page 49

E Listening I

See tapescript.

Page 50

F Vocabulary

1 *Equivalent words and phrases*

a) adverse b) shareholders c) dividends d) liabilities
e) heavy investment f) expand or bust!

2

Can't be right	Must be wrong
Express profit	Give the figure of
Only summarises	Simply draws conclusions about
Heavy investment in	Putting a large amount of capital into
Expand or bust	Make the company bigger or go down
Properly financed	Received enough investment
preferred to	Wanted

3 a) ratios b) adverse ratios c) profit
d) (current) liabilities e) percentage

4 a) foresee b) establish c) employed d) prefer
e) affect f) express

Page 51

G Discussion

a) He's going to attend a group meeting in Birmingham so he will need to explain all the problems relating to the ratios used by the finance people.
b) He'll have to explain the key ratios – for example, return on capital and how it will affect earnings per share. For this he will need to be able to explain how these things are calculated and why the return on capital in 1994 was so low.
c) The return on capital
d) The return on capital and the earnings per share
c) It's calculated as net profits as a percentage of the average capital employed during the financial year.
d) The low return on capital in 1994 was foreseen as part of the heavy investment in the Protocap Energy Saver. Also the Manara company was not properly financed to begin with, according to the Managing Director. The Group wanted them to borrow locally even though local interest rates were higher than in the UK. This is another reason why they had expected a lower return on capital.
g) The Group thought that the exchange risk was too great. They wanted Manara to borrow locally, even though local interest rates were higher than in the UK.

H Listening II

See tapescript.

Page 52

I Vocabulary

a) Customer receivables b) Group procedures
c) express d) to make them comparable with
e) working days f) our normal credit terms
g) free finance h) satisfactory i) considered acceptable
j) get this figure down to

J Grammar

1 a) Let's look at the inventories
b) Let's go over the balance sheet ratios.
c) Let's deal with the costing problems next.
d) Let's put this into our expansion plan.

Page 53

2 a) Let me see. In December 1991, our receivables were $550,000 and our sales for the year were $2.4 million.
b) Hang on a minute. That's 55 days of sales.
c) Just a moment. If our normal credit terms are 30 days, the customers are getting 25 days free finance from us!

3 a) The value of the contract was given in Deutschmark. (give)
b) Raw materials are shown in the balance sheet as part of the inventory.
c) Money owed to the bank is expressed as a liability.
d) The total value of production is given in dollars.
e) Volume of sales is expressed in metric tonnes.
f) Consumption of fuel is shown in litres.

4 a) If the road was blocked, there was no other way out.
b) If sales were $8,333 per day and receivables were $420 thousand we had 50.4 days of sales.

Page 54

5 *Connecting phrases*

a) So
b) *other* years *and with other* companies
c) *our* receivables *our* sales *and if we* assume
d) Even that
e) So, that means
f) *Well, we're still* ten days too high
g) comparisons *of this kind*
h) *All right, now* let's look at ....
i) .... so I'd be glad if you could ....
j) .... *these people* are getting ....
k) .... – *that's* $8,333 per day ....
l) What was the ratio for 1990? What's the average for the Group?
m) *I see.* So that means..........

Unit 5

Page 57
B Reading I
There are no fixed answers. The questions are meant for discussion. Consider the following:
Perhaps a solution can be found by looking at the profitability of each product made by Proteus.
How do accountants decide which products are more profitable and which products are less profitable?
As Managing Director, think of what could be done in the areas of production, finance and overheads.

Page 58
C Vocabulary
1 a) domestic b) develop c) reach d) carry out, undertake e) concentrate on f) review, (examine) g) obtain h) report back

2 a) directive – order
b) terms of reference – framework
c) the EC – the Common Market
d) costing – analysis of costs
e) procurement – finding and buying

3 In order: 1) desk research: 2) marketing targets; 3) financial targets; 4) product development

Page 59
D Grammar
1 a) The accountant said we should make more profit.
b) The boss said I should/was to work harder.
c) She said that we should not reduce the selling price.
d) The manager told them they were to increase sales.
e) The policeman said I was to pay a $500 fine.
f) The report concluded that Proteus should set up a joint venture subsidiary in Central Europe.

2 *Impersonal sentences*
a) It has been demonstrated that close relations can be established with ....
b) It is suspected that there /is/was/has been some corruption in the government.
c) It is feared that prices will go up this winter.
d) It is thought that most people do not like to live alone.
e) It has been proved some athletes /take/are taking/have taken drugs.
f) It is known that the sun will rise tomorrow.

Page 60
3 *Determiners*
(Note these rules are only summaries.)
a) You must use a determiner if you are referring to an object which (or a person who) is known or which you have in mind or which is unique.
b) You may, if you like, use a determiner if the object or person is general and the particularity is unimportant.
c) You must not use a determiner if it is a name or the generality of the person or object is unimportant.

The Financial Controller: refers to a unique individual
Proteus should reduce: zero determiner before names
sales of: sales in general
the Protocap and increase sales of: a unique product
other more profitable products: refers to existing but non-specific products
This advice goes against: the advice just mentioned
Group policy which wants: Group policy in general
sales of: sales in general
the Protocap to be boosted: a unique product

4 a) One among several directives
b) The normal rule requires *the* here. This exception is common *inside large organisations*, especially government departments.
c) The policy of the group as a whole, not a specific part of the policy
d) A unique product
e) The one and only product
f) the Proteus Group in particular
g) sales in general

Page 61
h) Names are not preceded by determiners.
i) *its* refers to the company Proteus. It specifies which target the writer is talking about.
j) *the* must be used before abbreviations: the USA, the UK, the EC etc. 'Made in USA', 'Made in UK', often found on product labels, is sub-standard English. Where the abbreviation is pronounced as a word, then it is treated like a name and no article is used: for example: UNPROFOR, UNESCO, INTERPOL, ASEAN, OPEC.
k) domestic competition in general
l) low margins in general

E Discussion
Note: To discuss many of the questions in this section you need to have studied Units 1 - 4.
...... The chief cause of Proteus troubles – the answer is debatable.
Choose from: falling profits despite increasing sales; low initial investment; low profitability of the Protocap; the need to expand to survive and the need for finance for expansion.

- The Proteus flagship product: the Protocap
- The gross profit margin in 1993: M$620,000 (See p. 17)
- The gross profit margin in 1994: M$650,000 (See p. 17)
- Subject of the directive: The Protocap should become the flagship product of Proteus and its sales should be increased.
- Reasons for fall in gross profit margin in 1994: Increased production overheads (warehousing and labour); short production runs; high setting up costs; low productivity of the Protocap; heavy initial investment in the Protocap (high finance costs); insufficient initial funding from Birmingham.

Aspects of the Protocap needing to be corrected: High production overheads (warehousing and labour costs); high setting up costs.
- Other aspects: low productivity of the Protocap; Sales could be increased, especially in Central and Eastern Europe, for which more investment is needed.
- Reason for not increasing selling price: heavy domestic competition (their competitors' prices are 2 per cent below theirs, see p. 38); low margins because of high production costs.
- The cause of planning problems in the factory: (See p. 42) Short production runs; long setting-up time; expensive planning and administration for each run.
- High unit costs: Expensive production costs. See above.
- Reduced cash flow: (See the Balance Sheet ratio receivables in Unit 4, Reading I, p. 45 and Listening II, p.51);
- Customers being given too much credit.
- Increased financial costs: high interest rates in Manara; heavy borrowing to finance production of the Protocap in 1994.
- Head office in Birmingham said that the Protocap was to be the Group's flagship product.
- Sales of the Protocap were to be boosted.
- The Manara subsidiary should increase its production. What the MD asked his managers to do:
- (See Unit 3, Listening III, p. 43) He wanted them to prepare plans for carrying out Head Office policy. The Financial Controller and Production Manager were to look for ways of reducing the costs. The Marketing Manager was to carry out research to find a Central or Eastern European market.

Advice of the Financial Controller:
- At first the Financial Controller advised that output of the Protocap should be reduced and that of other ordinary products increased. (Unit 1)
- Proteus will not be able to reach its target return on capital from sales in the EC because of strong competition.

Development of export markets:
- It was the only possible solution to the problem.
- Other parts of the world were covered by other Proteus subsidiaries.
- The task force was to boost sales of the Protocap.
- He asked the task force to do research and prepare plans for boosting sales of the Protocap in Central and Eastern Europe.
- Members of the task force: the Financial Controller, the Production Manager, the Marketing Manager.
- Responsibilities of the task force: competitors and business conditions, and to prepare plans for boosting sales of the Protocap in Central and Eastern Europe.
- Time to carry out their tasks: twenty-one days.

Page 63

G Vocabulary

1 a) .... we are worried about ....
b) .... because of the large ....
c) .... fall ....
d) .... understand the advantage ....
e) .... reduce ....
f) .... succeeds ....
g) .... conversion ....

2 a) offset/could offset/was able to offset b) local borrowings c) working capital d) foreign exchange e) prospects f) converted g) budget h) local currency i) earnings per share j) double taxation

3 *Use of prepositions*
a) interested *in*
b) worried *about*

Page 64
c) .... *for a change*
d) .... *with* the Chief Accountant
e) .... borrow *from* local banks
f) ....borrow *in* local currencies
g) .... the advantage *of* ....
h) .... fall *in* net profit.
i) The increase *in* ....

H Grammar

1 *Logical connectors*
a) contrast b) contrast c) addition d) sequencing e) reason f) contrast g) addition

Page 66

J Vocabulary

2 *Word families*

Noun	**Verb**	**Adjective**	**Adverb**
analysis	analyse	analytical	analytically
method	(use systematise)	methodical methodological	methodically methodologically
history	–	historical	historically
contribution	contribute	contributory	–
significance	signify	significant	significantly
activity	–	active	actively

Page 67

3 a) significant b) methods c) analyse d) contribution e) historical f) activities

4 *How synonyms are synonyms?*
a) *current (6) present (14)*
a current account; the present government; several people were present in the room; the current rate of growth; the current issue of the Accountancy Journal; 'That's all for the present, thank you.'
b) *examine (1) look at* (used in less formal situations)
We've looked at the causes of the delays; He examined the figures in great detail; At the end of the course, he was examined thoroughly on the subject; This morning we're going to look at some aspects of costing.
c) *decide (2) establish (20)*
The methods used to establish the true cost are incorrect; They decided to change the system; The company was established in 1864; The court

established the cause of death.

d) *calculate (23) work out (recalculate (5) = work out again)*
She worked out the answer on paper ; The engineer calculated the size of the beams needed for the building;
They worked out a solution to the problem.

e) *factor (24) influence (25)*
The profit margin was reduced due to several factors; The artist said there were several influences in his work.

f) *category (28) class*
They stayed in a top class hotel; There are several categories of cost driver at Proteus;
Arthur Ashe was a world class tennis player; The activities mentioned by the accountant are different categories of overhead.

g) *express (26) give (13)*
The figure was expressed as a percentage; He gave a large figure as the price he would pay; He gave his 'phone number; The first part was expressed in letters.

5 a) *Current* for continuous situations (the current war in Bosnia)
Present for immediate situations (the present crisis)

b) *Examine* for more formal and continuous situations
Look at for personal, immediate and less formal situations

c) *Decide* for personal and immediate situations
Establish for more formal situations

d) *Calculate* for more mathematical situations
Work out for personal, immediate and less formal situations

e) *Factors* are easily identified, discrete items.
Influences are larger and more general.

f) *Category* is used for in scientific and academic purposes.
Class may alos be used for in scientific and academic purposes but also has a much wider use (sport, biology, travel, for example).

g) *Express* is used when the writer/speaker wants to be mathematical.
Give is used much more generally.

Page 68

6 a) allocation b) reported c) resources d) forecast

7 a) reporting b) forecast c) source d) allocated

8 a) methodological errors b) allocation of overheads c) overstates d) reported costs e) corrected actual cost f) resources g) forecast h) budgeted cost i) cost driver

9

Material procurement	Material handling and storage
Production set-up	Maintenance
Quality control	Machinery department
Fitting department	Packing and despatch

10 *Formal and Informal*

Material procurement	Buying things
Production set-up	Getting ready to make
Quality control	Checking
Fitting department	Putting things together
Material handling and storage	Moving and keeping (also, warehousing)
Maintenance	Keeping in working order
Packing	Wrapping up
Despatch	Sending things

Page 70

L Grammar from Reading III

3 a) He did it by sacking half the workers.
b) He revived its finances using some accountancy software.
c) They rebuilt the warehouse taking several months to complete the job.
d) They did it by recycling the old building materials.

M Discussion

1 In the way overheads were allocated to products.
2 He recalculated the unit costs of two major products using activity costing methods.
3 He based them on activities such as production, buying, quality control, handling, storage and maintenance.
4 It significantly overstated the cost of the Protocap.
5 They were given as a percentage of labour expenditures (based on historical data).
6 Historical data
7 It didn't calculate the corrected actual cost of resources used in the production of a product.
8 They should establish the cost contribution of all the various activities to each unit, and then charge products their share of all the contributing activities.
9 This would be done by calculating the forecast or budgeted cost of each major activity and determining which product factor drove or influenced that activity.

Page 71

10 – 14 For examples of activities, see the list at the bottom of Reading, page 65.
For simplified explanations of activities, see J Vocabulary 10 at the bottom of page 68. But for more detailed descriptions ask your accountancy lecturer or a friend who is a qualified accountant.

15 They will visit departmental managers to find out which activities drive the costs arising in each department.

Unit 6

Page 76

C Vocabulary

1 a) acquisition b) a return c) formation d) mergers e) inherent

Page 77

2 a) merger b) formation c) acquisitions d) return e) inherent

3 *Noun phrases*
a) post-implementation audits b) third party c) fixed capital assets d) long term assets e) current investments f) long term borrowing g) existing businesses h) joint ventures

4 a) major b) adequate c) inherent d) effective e) current

Page 78
5 *Use of verbs*
a) leased b) apply to c) to rent d) count as e) carried out f) maintain

D Grammar
1 *Understood words*
a) of the money/of it
b) they had charged him / they had done so
c) title/one/book
d) of the invoice/of it

2 *Prepositions*
a) worth b) in c) on d) in e) post

Page 79
f) out g) within h) to i) for j) with k) (by) (through/with)

E Discussion
- A major project for Proteus: Acquisitions of fixed capital or long-term assets worth £100,000 or more, or the equivalent in other currencies.
- What they must take account of: the need to make an adequate return and country risks.
- Political risks (e.g. coups d'état, revolutions, strikes riots etc.)
- Economic risks (e.g. devaluation of payment currency, non-payment)
- Current investments: maintain effective control
  carry out post-implementation audits of new projects.
- cash purchases of fixed assets, leases of assets, construction of buildings, purchases of existing business, formations of new companies, through mergers or joint ventures
- Six

Pages 79 - 80
F Reading and activity
Evaluation of country risk:

More than 70 points:	Typical situation of an industrial nation with overall stability
55 – 70 points:	Country with moderate risks and certain impediments in daily operation
40 – 54 points:	High-risk country. Unfavourable business climate for foreign companies
Fewer than 40 points:	Not acceptable for foreign investment

Page 81
H Vocabulary
1 *Using adjectives*
Note: *financial* can be used with all the nouns in a) – e).
a) crucial b) proposed c) parent d) clear e) true

Page 82
Note: *certain* can be used with all the nouns listed.
f) potential g) strong h) annual i) product (used as an adjective in paragraph 4) j) adequate

2 a) crucial b) clear c) Financial d) latest e) Certain f) statutory

3 *Special terms*
a) annual accounts b) disclosure c) intellectual property rights d) unquantified claims e) product liability f) contingent liabilities g) statutory accounts h) borrowings guaranteed

Page 83
4 *Useful verbs*
a) faced b) finance c) persuade d) increase
e) provide f) treated g) disclose h) happened
i) occurred j) is considering k) have been made

5 *Lexical cohesion devices*
a) *lend money* (1.3) refers to finance in line 1.
b) *provides* (1.4) refers to lend in line 2.
c) *potential investors* (1.10) refers to *Whoever provides* and lender and provider.
d) *losses or expenses* (1.13) refer to contingent liabilities.

I Grammar
1 a) .... forced them to look for ....
b) The law requires public limited companies to show ....
c) ....urge the task force to find ....
d) They were compelled to ask the bank for a loan.

Page 84
2 a) ....as explained by the Financial Controller.
b) ....as demonstrated by the Accounts Manager
c) ....as prepared by the accountant.
d) ....as announced by the government ....

3 *Reference words*
a) They – the Proteus (Manara) Board
b) their – the parent company
c) They – contingent liabilities
d) the Group – the Group in Birmingham (1.5)
e) such claims – product liability and intellectual property rights (line 25).

J Discussion
- The crucial question: How to finance their proposed expansion
- Two possibilities for financing: borrowing from the bank or persuading the parent company to increase

its investment
- What the provider of the money will want to have: a clear and true picture of Proteus (Manara) Ltd's health as shown in the latest balance sheet
- What potential investors will want to see apart from the balance sheet: They'll want to know how a company's liabilities are treated.
- A strong influence on potential investors: the liabilities of the company
- Contingent liabilities: losses or expenses which might or might not happen depending on whether certain events occur
- Contingent liabilities shown in the balance sheet? No.
- Where contingent liabilities are disclosed: in a note in the Annual Accounts
- How contingent liabilities can be seen: They appear as borrowings guaranteed and 'other subsidiaries'.
- Examples: borrowings guaranteed and 'other subsidiaries'
- Examples mentioned: product liability and intellectual property rights

Unit 7

Page 90
C Vocabulary
1 a) a statement to the shareholders by the chairperson b) financial report c) Annual Report and Accounts d) Board of Directors Report e) Annual Accounts f) Auditor's Report

Page 91
4 a) publish b) reviews c) forecasts d) spread e) are required f) includes g) reports h) announced i) amounted to j) reflected k) faced l) depressed m) threatened/threatens n) is/are seeking

6 *Adjectives*
a) consolidated b) export, financial c) general, political d) political e) fresh f) major, financial g) fierce, political h) annual i) the previous j) the coming k) satisfactory l) stable m) substantial

Page 92
D Grammar
1 *The present simple*
1 In it he or she *reviews* the results of the past year and *forecasts* what will happen ....
so auditing work *is spread* evenly ....
Next *comes* the ....
which *is required* by law.
This *gives* an account of ....
The Annual Accounts *report* to shareholders on ....
and *show* the financial position at ....
The accounts are *followed by* ....
and *include* the following ....
The document also *includes* a summary of ....
and *gives* general information about ....
I *am* pleased to report ....
In our major export markets, we *face* fierce competition ....
which *depresses* our earnings and *threatens* the profitability of ....

2 *The passive*
a) The annual report was published last week.
b) The balance sheet has statement of money spent on research. (which was spent/which has been spent)
c) Expensive cars are given to the directors' families.
d) Earnings were/have been depressed by foreign competition.
e) Progress of the company is reflected in the growth of profits.

E Discussion
You may check your answers from Reading I (page 89).

G Vocabulary
2 a) optimistic tone
b) The higher earnings per share obscures a deterioration in the Group's cash position
c) Notes to the Accounts
d) exposure to fluctuations in .... foreign exchange rates
e) admitted
f) expansion into Europe was an option being considered
g) vehicle for further outward investment
h) to self-finance expansion solely from earnings
i) reluctant to contribute
j) Consequently the board.......... finance the expansion .... by borrowing
k) gearing
l) revising their profit forecast downwards

Page 95
4 a) deterioration in the Group's cash position
b) lower
c) was unwilling to
d) it will not be possible
e) deliver high dividends
f) by borrowing
g) revising .... downwards

5 a) borrowing up by 30 per cent
b) the most likely vehicle for .... outward investment
c) the Proteus company in Manara
d) outward investment
e) expansion

6 overseas

7 Financial catchphrases (given in order of use):
the optimistic tone of
faces a difficult future
are already encountering strong price competition

obscure a deterioration
fluctuations in exchange rates.
was an option being considered,
but was unwilling to go into detail.
It is well known, however,
in the present economic climate
Analysts reacted cautiously to
by revising their forecast of economic recovery downwards.

Page 96

9 *Useful adjectives*
a) economic b) exchange c) difficult d) the previous e) foreign f) optimistic g) price h) present i) total, present j) recent, (present) k) product

10 *Useful verbs*
a) financed b) show c) mean d) considered, went into e) went into f) worry g) rely on h) contributed i) face j) represented k) resulted in l) deliver

Page 97

11 all true

12 a) (i) b) (iv) c) (iv) (Note in the context of 'the Protocap range' (iii) is correct) d) (i)

Page 98

H Grammar

1 a) The flowers are already opening.
b) The rivers are already flooding.
c) The birds are already singing.
d) They are already digging the foundations.
e) Sales are already rising.

3 Note: While other tenses in the main clause are possible, using the present tense in *While* clause gives a stronger more permanent feeling.
a) While there are several ...., the Protocap is better ....
b) While .... the idea of .... seemed to be the .... in fact the situation is worse ....
c) While their governments set up an excellent ...., their industrial policies lead to pollution and other ....

Page 99

4 *Unless (present + future)*
a) It is difficult to do business in that country unless you find a partner.
b) Unless it rains soon, the plants will die.
c) Many people will die, unless help arrives soon.
d) Unless you service your car regularly, it will break down.
e) The shop will not take the video back unless you have the receipt.
f) Unless we go early, we will not get a seat in the restaurant.

Page 100

J Vocabulary

1 a) perform b) submitted c) appointed d) involves e) focused

2 a) official version b) statutory requirements c) audit layout d) auditing requirements e) trading licence f) satisfactory position g) Audit content h) head office i) financial records j) accounting staff

Page 101

K Grammar

Example D is not passive

1 a) .... will have to be found ....
b) .... will have to be filled in ....
c) .... will have to be shown ....
d) .... will have to be persuaded to ....
e) .... had to be signed ....
f) .... had to be repaired ....

2 a) After crossing the frontier, they ....
b) On hearing the new, they ....
c) Take the pills three times a day before eating.
d) When driving alone, he often ....

Unit 8

Page 104

C Vocabulary

1 a) plan b) board c) position d) markets e) sales f) marketing g) range h) rationalisation i) facilities j) costs k) strategy l) economies m) situation

Page 105

2 a) revised b) strategic c) strong d) permanent e) principal f) aggressive g) small h) profitable i) key j) fixed k) responsible l) preliminary m) emerging n) developing o) domestic p) stable q) political r) major

3 a) foresees b) to minimise c) will give d) occupies e) achieved f) selected g) was approved, has been approved will/may etc. be approved h) served i) targeted j) to implement

4 a) strategic ten-year plan *or* (less usual) ten-year strategic plan
b) the Proteus Group Board
c) return on capital

Page 106

d) highly profitable products
e) product research and development
f) the emerging market economies
g) stable political situation
h) base for expansion

5 a) product research and development b) base for

expansion c) emerging market economies d) ten year strategic plan e) return on capital f) stable political situation g) Proteus Group Board h) highly profitable products

Page 107
4 a) in b) on c) through d) in e) for f) with g) into

E Discussion
- The strategy of the Proteus Group:
  For subsidiary companies to export to allocated export markets. Each subsidiary to be responsible for a particular market.
- The task of subsidiary companies:
  To move rapidly to occupy strong and permanent positions in their principal markets.
- Strategy most recently approved by the Proteus Group Main Board:
  (Similar to the first question) Subsidiary companies are to move rapidly to occupy strong and permanent positions in their principal markets.
- What the subsidiary companies are required to do:
  To increase export sales by aggressive marketing in the countries they are responsible for.
- Expected annual increase in sales:
  Sales should increase by 10 per cent annually
- Expected annual growth in profits:
  Profits should grow by 15 per cent
- Expected return on profits for the first five years: 20 per cent
  Expected annual increase in sales for the second five years: 25 per cent
- Achievement of expansion:
  Through the aggressive marketing of a small range of highly profitable products, the targeting of key markets and profitable customers, a significantly higher investment in product research and development, and through the rationalisation of production facilities, to minimise fixed costs.
- Responsibilities assigned to Proteus Manara;
  Implementing the Group's strategy in Eastern Europe.
- The department of Proteus which has produced the Preliminary Plan: the Group Business Planning Department
- What the plan foresees:
  The upgrading of manufacturing facilities in Manara and the increase in sales volumes through entry into the emerging market economies of Central and Eastern Europe.
- How an increase in volume of sales will be achieved:
  Through entry into the emerging market economies of Central and Eastern Europe.
- How Proteus Manara should do this:
  By selecting the country with a developing domestic economy and stable politicial situation and that country could eventually serve as a base for expansion into all the major Eastern economies.
- How Proteus Manara should proceed:
  Same as above.
- The criteria for selecting a country as a base:
  It should have a developing domestic economy and a stable political situation. It would serve as a base for expansion into all the major Eastern economies.

Page 110
G Vocabulary
1 a) principle b) disclosure, publication c) obligations d) directives e) termination f) Income g) capabilities h) publication i) provisions j) assumption

2 a) the income-generating capabilities
  b) future strategies of corporate entities
  c) The Law shall apply to all participants on the market.
  d) The basic rules .... shall be in use in preparing reports and keeping the accounting records of entities.
  e) The Law shall apply to all participants on the market from whose operations persons and legal entities require information.
  f) These principles will be the basis for entities to declare their accounting policies and bases and will be in line with the generally accepted accounting policies (GAAP), international accounting standards and the Directives of the European Community.
  g) The last paragraph

Page 111
3 a) (vi) b) (ii) c) (vii) d) (viii) e) (i) f) (iv) g) (iii) h) (ii) i) (v)

H Grammar reference and practice
Page 112
1 a) .... to offset this year's profits for ....
  b) .... in preparing the Profit and Loss account.
  c) .... to obtain funds from their bank.
  d) In looking for gold in the mountains, the prospector ....

I Discussion
- The purpose of Law XVII of 1994 on Accounting: to lay down rules of content and disclosure
- What this law provides: basic rules for keeping financial records and accounts
- What the accounting regulations are in line with: International principles, GAAP and EC Directives
- The purpose of providing accounting information: to allow anyone to look at the accounts of a company
- Principles followed: International principles, GAAP and EC Directives
- Reason for following these principles: to provide a realistic and fair view of the income-generating capabilities of companies
- Information that should be provided by a business: net assets
- Other information: financial position
- Other information: future strategies
- Main purpose of the new law: to provide accounting

rules in line with international accounting principles
- What the law defines: the reporting of book-keeping obligations of business
- Obligations defined: the reporting of book-keeping obligations
- Principles defined: the principles to be applied in preparation of reports
- Requirements covered: those relating to disclosure, publication and auditing
- Whom the law applies to: businesses, public institutions
- Why it needs to lay down rules for such organisations: to provide a realistic and fair view of the income-generating capabilities of companies. Also to allow people to look at the accounts of a company.
- Whom in particular the law applies to: All types of business
- Anyone else? Public sector business (government-owned and financed companies)
- What the basic principles determined under Paragraph 15 will be used for; for preparing reports and keeping the accounting records of organisations.
- What companies should use the principle stated in the new law for: They can declare their own accounting policies.
- What the principles are in line with: Generally accepted accounting principles (GAAP), international standards and EC Directives
- The Principle of Going Concern: All annual accounts and company reports are produced on the assumption that the company is going to continue in business.

Page 115

K Vocabulary

1 a) consolidated balance sheet b) foreign currency borrowings c) long-term financing strategy d) exchange losses e) gearing f) fixed capital assets g) local currency assets

2 a) (iii) b) (i) c) (iii) d) (ii)

3 *Phrasal verbs*
a) sat in on b) report on c) borrow in d) forced down e) invest in f) took out g) setting up h) strengthened against

Page 116

4 i) – (d) ii) – (b) iii) – (c) iv) – (a) v) – (e)

L Grammar

2 *through*
  a) The government transformed the economy through privatisation.
  b) They marketed the product through their sales company in Kiev.
  c) Head Office is expanding into Eastern Europe through its subsidiary in Manara.

4 *First conditional*
  a) If interest rates fall, borrowing increases.
  b) If interest rates fall, we will borrow more from the bank.
  c) Gearing goes up, if companies raise loans.
  d) If we borrow now, our fixed costs will increase by a substantial amount.

Unit 9

Page 119

B Reading I

  a) The members of the Proteus Group (the shareholders)
  b) 31st December 1994
  c) 1st January – 31st December 1994
  d) Auditing Standards and the Companies Act 1985. (An Act is a law passed by Parliament.)

C Vocabulary

1 a) members b) view c) state of affairs d) fair e) Act
2 a) in accordance with b) state of affairs c) properly prepared

Page 120

3 You may check your answers against Reading I.

D Grammar

1 They head their report with the words: 'To the members of the Proteus Group plc'.
2 They use the present perfect tense: 'We have audited the accounts on page ....' and they say the accounts 'have been properly prepared ....' This tense carries the meaning of past action relating to the present.
3 Then refers back to the date just mentioned – 31/12/94.

Page 121

F Vocabulary

1 a) true b) fair c) required d) applicable e) inappropriate f) reasonable g) prudent h) inappropriate i) adequate

2 a) affairs b) period c) compliance d) format e) disclosure f) Act g) standards h) policy i) estimates j) company k) requirement l) records m) fraud n) irregularities

Page 122

3 a) is required b) be applied c) relate d) confirmed e) comply with f) maintains/maintained g) ensure h) safeguard, (maintain) i) prevent j) confirmed

4 a) required by law
  b) must be prepared in compliance with the required formats and rules for disclosure
  c) apply these consistently
  d) on a going concern basis
  e) comply with the above requirements

5 Check your answers against Reading II.

Page 123

G Grammar

1 *The passive*

a) .... the above requirements have been complied with/are complied with.

b) .... adequate accounting records have been maintained/were maintained/are maintained.

c) .... the requirements of the Companies Act 1985 have been/were/are complied with.

d) .... fraud and other irregularities should be prevented.

e) .... EC regulations have been/were/are conformed to.

f) .... certain rules must be observed.

2 *Relative clauses*

a) They have to follow rules which concern the preparation of the accounts.

b) The directors select the accounting policies which suit the needs of the company.

c) They must take account of the income and expenses which relate to the period being reported on.

d) The directors also confirm that the company has maintained accounting records which ensure that the accounts comply with the requirements of the Companies Act 1985.

e) They must also have records which safeguard the assets of the company and of the group.

Page 124

4 *Reported actions*

a) give b) had been prepared c) have been selected and applied d) are e) have been accounted for f) have been prepared

H Discussion

- The auditors' report is addressed to the shareholders.
- The auditors' report reports on the company's financial state of affairs and Annual Report
- What else? The company's Annual Accounts including the Profit and Loss Account
- Anything else? The company's Balance Sheet
- Standards referred to: Auditing Standards
- Other rules: the Companies Act 1985
- The responsibilities of the directors; They are required by company law to prepare accounts which give a true and fair view of the state of affairs of the company at the end of the financial year.
- Other responsibilities: The accounts must be prepared according to certain rules of format and disclosure. What others? They have to be prepared according to company law.
- What else? They have to observe accounting standards and select suitable accounting policies.
- Anything else? The accounts should represent a true and fair view of the state of affairs in the company. Their judgements should be reasonable and prudent.

Page 125

- Reasons why the directors have to do these things: They have to protect the assets of the company and prevent fraud and other irregularities.
- The view of the state of affairs of the company provided: A true and fair one.
- Period covered by the accounts: One year
- How the accounts should be prepared: With the required rules and formats for disclosure
- The rules they take into account: Accounting rules
- Other requirements: Company law
- What else: Selected accounting policies
- Anything else? The Companies Act 1985
- What the accounting records ensure: That the accounts comply with the law
- The purpose of the Companies Act 1985: To protect the assets of the company
- Another purpose: To prevent fraud
- Anything else? To prevent other irregularities

Page 126

J Vocabulary

1 a) historical cost convention g) rate of exchange
b) applicable UK accounting standards h) exchange differences
c) associated company i) reserves
d) external customers j) depreciation
e) foreign currency asset k) write-off
f) the results l) estimated useful life

2 a) reviews b) treat .... as c) was incorporated

Page 127

d) was carried at cost e) was written off
f) include .... in ....

3 a) historical b) applicable, accounting, associated c) audited, subsidiary, associated d) subsidiary, associated e) invoiced f) external g) sales h) trade i) foreign j) overseas k) average l) fixed, tangible m) tangible n) estimated o) commercial p) technological q) normal, useful r) manufacturing s) realisable

4

convention	custom
standards	measure of quality
turnover	annual income
discount	rebate
depreciation	percentage reduction
freehold	completely owned property
obsolescence	becoming out of date
wear and tear	deterioration through use

Page 128

K Grammar

a) under b) with c) into d) at e) from f) at g) during

L Discussion

- The basis of preparation of accounts:

The historical cost convention and compliance with all applicable UK accounting standards
- The convention the accounts prepared under: The historical cost convention
- What the historical cost convention is: Pricing everything at original cost
- What the accounts of a group of companies incorporate: They incorporate the audited assets and liabilities of subsidiary companies and the group's share of associated companies for the year.
- Turnover: Turnover is goods and services invoiced during the year to external customers and associated companies
- What is excluded from turnover: Value added tax and other sales taxes, less trade discounts
- How foreign currency and liabilities are shown in the balance sheet: They are translated into sterling at rates of exchange ruling on balance sheet date.
- How the results of overseas subsidiary and associated companies are translated: They are translated using average rates of exchange.
- How exchange adjustments are dealt with: Exchange adjustments arising directly from the translation of balance sheet items are taken directly to reserves.
- How tangible fixed assets are handled: They are carried at cost less depreciation.
- How is depreciation normally applied? It is normally calculated so as to write off the cost of fixed assets (except freehold land) evenly over their estimated useful lives.
- What is taken into account when calculating the useful life of an asset: Commercial and technological obsolescence as well as normal wear and tear are taken into account.
- How research and development expenditure is treated: Research and development expenditure, other than on fixed assets, is treated as a charge against revenue in the year in which it is spent.
- How stocks are treated: They are included in the accounts either at cost (including manufacturing overheads, where appropriate) or net realisable value, whichever is the lower.

Page 129

N Vocabulary

1 a) liberalisation process b) iron grip c) The Chancellor of the Exchequer d) remit dividends e) It's not all a bed of roses. f) The authorities here are going in the right direction. g) repatriated dividends h) withholding tax

Page 130

2 *Different kinds of tax*
a) sales b) corporation c) value added tax
d) withholding e) penalty

3 a) withdraws capital b) repatriate c) Autumn Budget d) allowances e) subject to f) special duties g) standard rate h) luxury goods

Page 131

P Vocabulary

1 a) The tax situation in Barakonia is not very encouraging to the foreign investor.
b) .... featherbed all the Barakonians who are not accustomed to unemployment
c) .... making as much of the workforce as possible redundant
d) .... not all business expenses are tax deductible
e) .... depreciated on a straight line basis
f) remitting dividends on investment
g) You have to take a long term view.
h) .... (on) a reducing balance over (.......... years)

Unit 10

Page 134

C Vocabulary

1 *Verbs*
a) is aiming, aims b) established
c) are concentrating on d) generate

Page 135

e) was developed f) source g) is distributed
h) achieved i) obtained j) was appointed

2 *Nouns*
a) mission b) objectives c) potential d) maintenance
e) development f) technology g) laboratory
h) selection i) expertise j) sourcing
k) distributorships

Page 136

3 *Adjectives*
a) permanent b) dominant c) major d) high value
e) extensive f) exclusive g) neighbouring h) rigorous
i) local j) key k) intensive l) continuous
m) managerial n) long-term o) substantial

4 *Linked words*
a) dominant position
b) generate high profit margins
c) extensive value added services in the areas of maintenance, training and development
d) low-cost manufacturing
e) subsidiary companies
f) rigorous selection
g) increase local sourcing of key materials
h) develop local managerial and technical skills in order to reduce labour costs and the dependence on imported expertise
i) key market
j) dominant position is attainable

Page 137

5 a permanent position (distributorship)
exclusive distributorship (position)
high value products (skills)

key markets (distributorship, skills)
labour costs
low cost manufacturing
neighbouring countries
subsidiary companies
substantial potential, costs
technical skills (distributorship)

D Grammar

1 *in order to*

a) *To achieve* is not a main verb. To make it grammatically complete, it would have to begin for example: *We aim to achieve ....*, where *We* is the subject and *aim* is the main verb.

b) To obtain full management control of ....
To establish exclusive distributorships in ....
To increase the degree of 'nationalisation' of ....

2 A expresses the future.
B, C and D express intention.

3 through (lines 8, 11, 23)

Page 138

E Before Reading

a) For the Proteus Head Office Finance Department.
b) Proteus (Manara) Ltd
c) Proteus was considering acquiring Elektra.
d) The staff needed retraining and probably their methods needed to be brought up to date.

Page 139

G Vocabulary

1 a) headed b) reports c) have excellent experience d) manually e) re-entry of data f) laid down g) prescribes

2 a) staffing – workers, staffing, recruitment, personnel management
b) software – programme, process, data, application, systems
c) statistics – numbers, distribution, average

3 a) paragraph 1: department, section heads
paragraph 2: systems
paragraph 4: companies, department, office
b) paragraph 1: the Chief Accountant, the General Manager, the section heads
paragraph 2: run
c) paragraph 3: Law, requires, prescribes, should be used, should be submitted
paragraph 4: must end

Page 140

I Vocabulary

1 a) set b) maintains c) are summarised d) are transferred e) is produced f) are carried out g) amounts to h) ensure i) maintain j) achieve k) are checked l) to compute m) collecting n) had been paid over o) facilitates

Page 141

2 a) mandatory (obligatory) b) limited c) control d) accounting e) specific f) summarised g) Internal h) statutory i) a formal j) chief k) annual l) crucial (essential, critical)

3 a) Balance Sheet b) Profit Statement c) The industrial costing section d) unit costs e) Day Books f) Sales and Purchase ledgers g) Central Accounting Book h) Nominal or General Ledger i) Monthly trial balance j) Auditing and Internal Control k) desk review l) Statutory financial reports

J Grammar

1 The passive

1 The identity of the person who did the action is unimportant: B,C
2 The writer wishes to focus on the object of the action: A,J
3 Combination of 1 and 2: D,E,F,G,H,I,K,L

3 The example in Reading III is in lines 15 – 16:
It amounts to little more than a desk review ....

Page 143

4 While/as

A at the same time B because

5 Either/or

Grammatically, all meanings are possible. So we have to derive the meaning from the context of the Report. In any case, the form used here is highly ambiguous.

Meaning a) This is most unlikely because, if it was important, the Financial Controller had only to find out.
Meaning b) This is improbable but possible.
Meaning c) This seems the most likely explanation
Note: a fourth meaning is possible:
d) The reports were sometimes sent to one department and sometimes to the other.

K Discussion

- Head of Elektra's Accounting Department: the Chief Accountant
- The sections of the accounting department: Financial Accounting, Payroll, Industrial Costing and Inventory Control
- The Financial Controller's comment on the section heads: They have excellent experience of their own sections, but little knowledge of the work of the others.
- The equipment of Elektra's accounting department: A small minicomputer
- The reason why the central accounting system is run manually: No software is available to process data from the minicomputer without re-entry of data.
- The controls in operation; The National Accounting Law No. 420, which requires companies of the size of Elektra to maintain a double entry system and prescribes in great detail what accounts should be

used and what reports should be submitted.

- The Barakonian financial year ends on December 31st.
- Is this the case in Western countries? No. Companies' financial years end at different times.
- What happens to most reports: They are sent either to the Barakonian Central Planning Department or the National Statistics Office.
- The problem posed by the way information about unit costs is presented: It is not presented in a way to facilitate decisions on selling prices.
- Price setting: They were set by the Barakonian Central Planning Agency while in the West they are set by management.
- What is produced from the Day Books: Personal Accounts for customers' and suppliers' accounts.
- Where all the information is collected: In the Central Accounting Book
- The UK equivalent to the Central Accounting Book: The Nominal or General Ledger
- What is derived from the Central Accounting Book: Monthly trial balances
- Elektra's annual audit is carried out by the chief accountant of a neighbouring company during a one-week period in March.
- What the Financial Controller says about the annual audit: It amounts to little more than a desk review of the statutory financial reports to ensure their compliance with the law.
- What else he says: There is no formal audit according to UK or international standards, although there is some internal control activity.
- Elektra's controls: The Inventory Control section personally carry out checks on levels of stock items which are critical to the achievement of production targets. But the Payroll Department checks its own records each month to ensure that wages are correctly computed.
- How they ensure that wages are correctly computed and all taxes are collected and paid over to the Tax Office: This is done by the Payroll Department. They check their own records each month to ensure that wages are correctly computed and all taxes are collected and paid over to the Tax Office.

Glossary

This glossary covers the main terms used in this book. It does not aim to cover accounting terms in areas outside the scope of this book. Some terms are interchangeable or are used loosely in practice to have the same meaning (e.g revenue and income; profit and margin; costs, expenses and charges). Other terms have different meanings within English-speaking countries (debtors [UK] is the same as receivables [USA]: again, US practice uses the term income to mean sales revenue and profit.

Accounting period The period covered by a company's financial statements

Accounting policies The general rules for preparing accounting statements

Accounting ratios Methods used to measure a company's financial performance, using its financial statements

Accounting Standards General rules which set mandatory levels of precision and presentation of financial statements. In the UK such standards are set by the accounting profession, while in other countries such standards are set out in a law or directive. See International Accounting Standards.

Activity based costing A method of charging labour and overhead costs based on the activities comprising the manufacturing and distribution of a product or service

Administration costs All costs involved in the administration of a company, not relating to the cost of sales. Examples : accounting, administration, human resources and general management

Annual audit The examination of the records and accounting statements of a company by independent, external auditors. In some countries an annual audit is obligatory for all companies, while in others smaller companies are exempt. In the UK it is also called the statutory audit because a law or statute requires it.

Annual Report The principal report which a company presents to its shareholders, usually based on the audited annual financial statements

Assets What a company or organisation possesses in physical (tangible) form or in the form of intangible items such as rights, patents.

Audit Report A report issued by auditors. Normally independent, external auditors will issue an Audit Report after examination of a company's annual financial statements. The term can also include reports on other auditing work done, either by independent auditors or by the internal audit department (usually of large companies).

Audit testing Tests carried out by auditors to ensure that a company's systems are properly used and secure and that all transactions are correctly recorded and valued

Auditing Standards Regulations governing the professional work of auditors in a country

Auditors Professional accountants who specialise in the examination of financial records and systems

Balance Sheet The statement of assets and liabilities of a company at the end of an accounting period

Balance Sheet ratios Comparative measures of a company's financial strength and liquidity based on the Balance Sheet

Bank balance The balance of cash held in a bank account

Board of Directors The senior management team of a company, appointed by the shareholders

Break-even point	The point or level of business activity at which the income from a product is equal to the total of the fixed and variable costs
Budget	A plan expressed in money terms. For a business it is a comprehensive financial plan, normally for the twelve months ahead.
Budgeted cost	A planned cost, used to control expenses
Capital	The money or other assets with which a company starts in business. The accumulated wealth of a company
Capital employed	The funds or wealth used by a company for its operations. It can be defined in several ways according to the purpose of the calculation. Normally, it is taken as the total assets less the short-term liabilities.
Cash flow	The difference between the cash received and cash spent during a company's operations
Cash flow statement	A statement showing the cash receipts and payments in a period. This term is also used to describe the statement of Sources and Applications of Funds.
Cash position	The amount of cash (and cash equivalents) recorded in a company's books at a moment in time
Cash equivalents	Assets which can be can be converted into cash at short notice (e.g. 4-5 days)
Central Bank	The senior bank of a country. Its main function is to regulate the banking system. In some countries it is controlled directly by the government. In others it is independent of central government (e.g. the US Federal Reserve).
Chairman	The person (usually also a Director) who presides over a controlling body. In Proteus plc, he presides over meetings of shareholders and of the Board of Directors.
Chairperson	A neutral term describing both male or female persons who preside over a board, committee or organisation
Chancellor of the Exchequer	The British Minister of Finance
Charge against revenue	An expense or cost which is deducted from income
Chart of Accounts	A list of all the accounts which comprise the Balance Sheet and Profit and Loss statements. Each account is usually identified by a numerical code. See also Nominal Ledger Codes.
Chartered Accountant	UK term denoting an accountant who has been admitted (by examination) to membership of the oldest UK professional accounting body, established by Royal Charter
Closing Inventory	The value of the inventory (or stock) at the end of an accounting period
Code	In accounting this means a short series of numbers or alpha-numeric characters (usually not more than 8 characters) used to refer quickly to a larger field containing data or a description. Example : code 0001 – Plant and Machines (at cost).
Collateral	A form of additional security which guarantees or otherwise assures to a creditor that all amounts payable under the loan contract will be duly paid. Can take the form of a guarantee or the pledging of an asset.
Commercial and technological obsolescence	The process by which products are superseded in the market for commercial reasons (lower price, better service) and by technological factors (more modern or more efficient products)
Consolidated Accounts	The accounts of a group of companies combined into one set of accounts
Consolidated Balance Sheet	The statement showing the assets and liabilities of a parent company and its subsidiaries
Consolidated Profit and Loss Account	The statement of the income, expenses and profit of a parent company and its subsidiaries

Contingent liability Liabilities which are dependent on a condition which exists at the balance sheet date and which will happen only if a particular event occurs or fails to occur. They are shown in the notes to the annual accounts, but not in the Balance Sheet.

Corporation Tax UK term to describe the tax charged on the profits of a corporation (limited company)

Cost accounting The branch of accounting which records and analyses the costs of products, services, activities in order to measure their profitability or productivity

Cost Centre Code A numerical or alpha-numerical code which identifies a cost centre, a place or an activity, to which costs and income can be allocated. Example : a production department, the maintenance service.

Cost driver A factor (usually non-financial) which drives or influences a cost. For example the cost of a single Quality Control inspection is determined by the number of inspections in a period.

Cost driver rate A rate per unit of activity, found by dividing the total cost of that activity by the number of activities of the cost driver. For example, if the total overhead expense of Quality Control is £1,500 and there are 300 inspections, then the cost driver rate for each inspection is £5.00.

Cost of sales The sum of all costs incurred to bring a product to the point when it can be sold to a customer. In a manufacturing company these costs will typically include all material, labour and overhead costs in the factory. See also Operating Expenses.

Costing The practice of identifying and accumulating costs relating to the cost of sales and to the valuation of stock

Costing module Refers to software which processes costing data. A group or set of computer programs, normally part of a company's accounting software system.

Costing system A system for organising categories of costs and procedures in order to accumulate costs relating to the cost of sales and to the valuation of stock

Country Risk A risk or threat which is specific to one country. It may be political, social, or environmental.

'Crash' sale A sale carried out under conditions of pressure and difficulty, and at great speed

Creditors Persons or entities which are owed money or value

Cross guarantee Mutual guarantee given by a creditor and a debtor, of lender and borrower, to ensure that each will fulfil his obligations under a contract

Currency The money in general use in a country

Current assets Assets with a life of less than 12 months

Current assets – Inventories Inventories are current assets because they should be 'turned over' several times in a year, that is they should have an average life of less than 12 months.

Current assets – Receivables Amounts owed by customers and due to be paid within 12 months

Current assets – Bank Balances Denotes cash in hand, in bank and deposit accounts (in any currency), and funds available at short notice.

Current liabilities Liabilities to be settled/paid within 12 months

Current liabilities – Payables Amounts payable to suppliers and creditors

Current liabilities - Tax payable on profits Amounts assessed by a tax authority for payment or amounts provided for future tax liabilities

Current liabilities – Short-term Loans Bank overdrafts, loans from banks or other (non-trade) creditors repayable repayable within the next 12 months

Current liabilities – Other taxes payable Any taxes which are not taxes on profits, e.g. social security taxes, personal taxes withheld from employees' salaries, property taxes

Customer receivables Amounts owed by customers in payment of normal invoices or other trade debts. Also called trade debtors

Day Books Books which register each day's accounting transactions, e.g. sales invoices, purchase invoices. This term relates mainly to manual book-keeping systems. In computer systems, a day book is simply a list of daily accounting transactions.

Debt An amount owed by a debtor to a creditor

Debtors Persons or entities which owe money to creditors

Depreciation The systematic reduction in the value of an asset to show the effect of usage and obsolescence. See straight line depreciation and reducing balance depreciation.

Desk research Research carried out at one's desk, i.e without leaving the office

Desk review A review (of a report or project) carried out at one's desk

Directive A general instruction or command. In the context of this book, we refer to 'EU Directives' which are instructions issued by the EU Commission to the governments of EU member states. These directives have the force of law and member states must introduce them as a law or a regulation.

Directors' responsibilities for the accounts Directors of certain companies subject to the UK Companies Acts are considered to have definite responsibilities for the financial statements, and include in the published Annual Accounts a statement describing their responsibilities.

Disclosure The presentation of information which a law or regulation requires to be made available to interested parties such as shareholders, employees, bankers and creditors

Discount An amount which is deducted from another amount, e.g. a sales discount is deducted from the gross value of sales, yielding a 'net' sales figure.

Diversification Investing in different business activities, e.g a retailer who invests in production

Domestic competition Competition within a company's *domestic* or *home* market

Double taxation The taxation of profits in more than one country

Duties This can mean either obligations or responsibilities or payments to tax authorities e.g. customs duty on imported goods.

Earnings per share The net profit divided by the average number of shares on issue during the accounting period

Economic liberalisation The elimination of economic restrictions (such as tariff barriers), with the aim of expanding or modernising a country's economic system

Emerging market economies Refers to countries in the process of adopting a market economy such as the former COMECON countries and underdeveloped countries moving to a full market economy.

Employment policy The policy towards employment of staff, and their working conditions.

Entrepreneurs Persons who undertake a business or enterprise with the chance of profit or loss. Directors and managers of commercial businesses

Equity The issued share capital plus reserves which represent the investment in in a company of the shareholders

Estimated useful life The period during which an asset will help to create wealth for a company at the end of which it will have no value. A term used in relation to depreciating an asset, when deciding how to charge production with the original cost of acquiring it

EU, The The European Union

Eurodollar An US Dollar held in a bank in Europe

European Union Formerly known as the EEC (European Economic Community) and also known as 'The Common Market'. The economic and political association of various European countries as a unit with internal free trade and common external tariffs. Founded by the Treaty of Rome 1957

European Community Directives Rules established by the Commission of the European Union (EU) which must be adopted by all EU member countries either through a law or regulation.

Exchange losses Losses suffered when translating the results of foreign exchange transactions into a particular currency ('realised loss'), or when translating the net assets of a company into another currency (an 'unrealised loss')

Exchange rate The value of one currency in terms of another

Exposure Refers to the risk of loss or some business or economic danger.

Factory overheads Costs which relate to manufacturing operations and which are not labour and material costs

Financial accounting The classification and recording of the monetary transactions made by an entity, and the presentation of the results of those transactions and of the entity's financial position at the end of the accounting period

Financial costs Any cost which is shown in the Profit and Loss statement as a deduction from income in computing profit, i.e. expenses, allocated costs, non-cash expenses such as depreciation and provisions

Financial records The records of an entity, including the documents for each transaction, the books of account (ledgers) and the financial statements

Financial targets Targets of financial performance which must be met, e.g. sales, profits, return on capital, dividend per share

Financial year The official accounting period of an entity. In some countries this is determined by law, e.g. January 1- December 31. In other countries companies may select any month in which to end their accounting year.

Finished goods Goods which are ready for despatch to customers

Fixed asset An asset which has an estimated useful life of more than 12 months. Such long-term assets will be *tangible* (machines) or *intangible* (patents).

Fixed assets – capital assets The same as fixed assets (above). More often used in US accounting

Fixed assets – land and building Freehold or leasehold land and buildings which have been acquired by a company

Fixed assets – plant and equipment Machinery, equipment, factory and office furniture and fittings

Fixed capital acquisitions The acquisitions of ownership (and use) of fixed assets through purchase from suppliers or by constructing them using a company's own resources and labour. Note that a company may acquire the use of fixed assets by leasing or renting them.

Fixed costs Costs which remain at approximately the same level, whatever the level of sales or business activity

'Flagship' product The ship on which an admiral flies his flag. Here the term means the leading or most important product of a company.

Foreign currency assets Assets held in foreign countries or denominated or valued in terms of a foreign currency

Foreign currency borrowings A borrowing of an amount which is expressed in a foreign currency, usually in a foreign country but can be borrowed in the country of the reporting entity, e.g. Eurodollars borrowed in the UK by a UK company

Foreign exchange The currency of another country. Also means the process of dealing in currencies of other countries

Formal audit An audit for some specific purpose, e.g. an annual audit, or the verification of a specific fact, asset or valuation.

GAAP Generally Accepted Accounting Principles

Gearing The relationship between the two major types of long-term finance available to companies – borrowing and investment by shareholders.

Gross margin The difference or surplus after deducting the cost of sales from the net sales income. Same as 'gross profit'

Gross profit Same as 'gross margin'

Group Board or Group Main Board A UK term describing the Board of Directors of the 'parent' or 'holding' company of a group of companies. See Main Board.

Group Chairman The Chairman who presides over the Board of Directors of a parent or holding company

Group Export Manager The senior manager of a group of companies responsible for all exporting operations

Group Financial Director The senior financial officer who is a member of the Board of Directors of a group

Group guidelines Any instructions which all subsidiary companies must follow

Group of companies A group of companies which are controlled by a parent company either though shareholding or management contract

Head Office A popular expression to denote the controlling organisation (or parent company) of a group of companies

Hedge An action to control, reduce or minimise an exposure or risk which might cause a loss or expense, e.g. against losses due to changes in foreign exchange rates.

Historical cost The actual cost of acquiring assets, goods and services

Historical cost convention The generally accepted practice or agreement that all financial transactions shall be recorded at their original, actual value or cost of acquisition

Historical data Actual data which relates to present or past periods, as opposed to future or forecast data

Industrial costing The system of recording and accounting for all costs in an industrial or manufacturing process

Intangible asset A non-physical asset, e.g. a right, a license, a trade mark, a patent

Intellectual property A type of intangible asset. Property which derives its value from intellectual activity and from demand for the asset itself

Interest costs Costs associated with payment of interest on loans

Internal control Systems for the control of business and financial activities, the protection of assets, rights, records

Internal management reporting Systems of reporting to a company's management team, rather than to outside persons (shareholders) or outside bodies (government)

International Accounting Standard Standards for accounting set by the International Accounting Standards Committee (IASC), which includes representatives from most major countries. They have no legal effect or force but provide a universal code of reporting practice.

Inventories Materials used in the manufacturing or selling operations of a business, (UK : 'stock'). Also used in the singular

Inventory control The system of managing the acquisition, storage, movement and recording of inventories

Investment Putting money or other resources into a business activity on a long-term basis

Joint venture A commercial operation based on a formal agreement between two companies to collaborate for achieving a common business aim

Labour costs Costs associated with the employment of labour in a company's operations

Land and buildings Refers to land and buildings, which are shown in a company's Balance Sheet, being either owned or on a long-term lease.

Law relating to disclosure publication A law which governs what information must be shown or 'disclosed' by a company in its Annual Accounts or other specified document

Ledger A book, specifically an accounting record, which is organised so as to show financial information in an appropriate manner

Ledger – Sales The 'book' or ledger which records all financial transactions with customers

Ledger – Purchase Ledger The ledger which records all transactions with suppliers and other creditors

Ledger – Nominal Ledger The ledger which records all financial transactions of a company in an analytical form and from which the data for the two main financial statements (Balance Sheet and Profit and Loss Account) are directly drawn. In some countries it is called the 'analytic' ledger.

Ledger – General Ledger Another name for the Nominal Ledger, derived from the fact that it provides a *general* view of the financial position and results of a company

Local currency borrowings Money borrowed in the currency of the country

Long-term asset acquisitions Any acquisition of a long-term asset, whether purchased using own funds or through financing, e.g. lease purchase

Long-term financing strategy A plan describing the methods and amounts required to finance a company's operations over a long period, e.g. 5-10 years

Main board The highest or most senior board of directors of a group of companies. See Group Main Board.

Maintenance The process of keeping an asset or system in good operating condition

Management accounts The provision of financial information for the management of a company. Usually based on the financial statements, management accounting reports interpret and evaluate these statements as an aid in the management decision-making process.

Managing Director The senior executive director of a company. Known in the USA as Chief Executive Officer (CEO), he is functionally responsible for the other directors who are members of the board.

Manufacturing overheads Overhead costs (not labour and materials) relating to the manufacturing process

Margin The difference between income and costs. Same as 'profit'.

Market penetration The successful entry into a market by a company through achieving sales of its goods or services

Market share The ratio of a company's sales in a particular market expressed as a percentage of the total estimated sales of that market

Marketing targets Elements of a plan for marketing which must be accomplished, e.g. carrying out research into specific markets, areas or segments.

Material cost The invoice price of materials acquired; used for determining unit costs and the valuation of inventory. Can also include other costs relating to the acquisition of materials, e.g. procurement, receipt, inspection, storage.

Material handling and storage The activity of handling materials, including receipt and inspection of materials delivered by suppliers, the rejection of defective items, the physical handling storage of materials during and after production, prior to despatch to customers

Material procurement The activity of obtaining materials for an entity, involving the location and selection of suppliers, the negotiation of terms, the receipt of delivered goods

Memorandum ('Memo') An internal written communication. Also a formal letter between two persons or companies to record a meeting or an agreement, e.g. Memorandum of Understanding

Merger The bringing together of two or more companies, by creating a new company, to which each merging company sells its assets

Multinational	A company which does business in many countries, either through exporting, subsidiary companies or joint ventures
Net assets	See Balance Sheet – Net Assets. Total assets less current liabilities. Also denotes Capital Employed.
Net profit	Profit after tax. Also profit available for distribution as dividends or transfer to reserves.
Net profit as a percentage of sales	The ratio of net profit to sales, an indicator of the profitability of a company
Nominal Ledger	See 'Ledger – Nominal Ledger'.
Nominal Ledger Codes	These are numerical or alpha-numerical codes which identify specific accounts in the Nominal or General Ledger. See also Chart of Accounts.
Notes to the accounts	Explanations of items shown in the financial statements of a company, either to inform interested parties or to disclose information required by a law or regulation. Examples: details of purchase, sales and depreciation of fixed assets.
Offset	Using one value to reduce the effect of another contrary value, e.g. A owes B £ 100, and B owes A £150. B reduces his debt to A by the £100 which A owes to him and pays A the net amount of £50.
Opening inventory	Inventory or stock at the beginning of the accounting period
Operating expenses	All expenses arising from a company's operating activities. These could include manufacturing expenses, but accounting statements tend to separate these from all other expenses, showing them as a component of the cost of sales, when computing the gross profit. The expenses described below are reported as operating expenses – e.g. marketing, selling, distribution, development, administration. Interest expense and income are normally shown as Financing Activities.
Operating expenses – Administration	Normally includes expenses such as legal, personnel (Human Resources), accounting, general management.
Operating expenses – Selling	Selling expenses can relate solely to sales activities, but sometimes include marketing expenses.
Outward investment	Investment outside the investing company. e.g. to a subsidiary company
Overheads	All expenses except for labour or material costs
Overhead allocation	The allocation of overhead expenses to different activities, departments, products of a company in order to show how much each one costs to run
Parent company	A company which has a controlling interest in another, through shareholding or by management control
Payables	Liabilities to pay debts or dues
Payroll	The system for calculating and paying salaries, wages and related taxes
Payroll department	The department responsible for paying wages and salaries
Penalty, tax penalty	A payment imposed by a taxation authority for an offence against the tax laws or regulations
P/E ratio	Price earnings ratio. The market price of a company's shares divided by the earnings (or profit) per share
Personal accounts	The financial record of transactions with individual persons or companies, such as suppliers, customers
Plant and equipment	Machines, fittings, equipment used in the production process of a business
Post-implementation audit	A review or evaluation of the financial or operational effect of an investment, project or event, to verify if the expected results were achieved
Prime cost	The total cost of direct material and direct labour
Principal	A person or company which is acting on its own behalf and is not contracted by another
Principle	A general rule

Principle of Going Concern A fundamental accounting principle which states that the net assets shown in a company's published financial statements are valued on the basis that the company will continue to trade normally in the foreseeable future

Procurement The obtaining of goods or services e.g. by purchase, rental or leasing

Product Used to refer to goods or to services, e.g. a bank often describes its services as 'products'

Product cost The cost of a finished product built up from its cost elements

Productive assets Assets used in the production process, as opposed to 'non-productive assets' which are either inactive or used on non-productive processes

Production targets Specific objectives of a production department, e.g. units to produce in a day or week

Profit The increase in the net assets of a company, or the balance remaining after deducting all expenses and taxes from the invoiced sales of a company

Profit, gross profit Profit after deducting the cost of sales from the net revenue

Profit, operating profit The profit after deducting the cost of sales and all expenses of the company's operations, such as selling and administration, but before considering any financial expenses or income

Profit, profit before tax The profit remaining after deducting all expenses of the company's operations and which is now subject to tax

Profit, net profit Profit after tax but before it is used to pay dividends or make transfers to reserves

Profit, profit available for distribution Similar to net profit (above)

Profit and Loss Statement The explanation of the financial results of the company's operations during during the accounting period under review, e.g. a month or a year

Profit contribution Used in describing 'marginal' costing, and refers to the amount of profit contributed by a product or business area to cover or pay for the fixed expenses of a company. The contribution is calculated by deducting all variable costs from the sales figure.

Profit forecast A prediction of the expected profit for a future accounting period

Profit and Loss Account See Profit and Loss Statement

Profit and Loss Account ratios : Measures of operational profitability and efficiency

Factory overheads Factory overhead expenses are compared with sales and with direct labour costs

Gross profit Gross profit is calculated as a percentage of sales

Material costs Material costs are calculated as a percentage of the total cost of sales and also of total invoiced sales.

Selling expenses Selling expenses are computed as a percentage of sales, although in some companies they are shown as a percentage of gross profit.

Administrative expenses Administrative expenses will be shown as a percentage of sales.

Public limited company (Plc) A term applied in the UK to limited companies whose shares are traded on a principal national stock exchange, e.g. the London Stock Exchange

Purchases Acquisition of goods or services used in a company's operations

Quality control A management system to ensure that a company's products, services and materials reach certain standards of quality and excellence.

Quarterly Management Meeting Refers to the meetings of Proteus management every three months

Raising capital Seeking and obtaining cash investments from current and potential shareholders in exchange for the issue of shares in the company

Rationalisation Reorganising a company's activities, usually to reduce costs

Raw materials The basic materials used in the process of manufacturing a product

Receivables Money owed by customers for goods supplied on credit or amounts expected to be received from other debtors

Recession Temporary decline in national economic activity or prosperity

Reducing balance depreciation An asset may be assumed to lose more of its value in the earlier years. A higher charge may be made in the first years through selecting a higher percentage than under the straight line method and applying it to the reduced balance (the original cost less depreciation already charged). Example : a car may cost US$ 10,000. In year 1 the depreciation charge may be 30% on the cost, leaving a reduced balance of US$ 7,000. In year 2, 30% is applied to the US$ 7,000 giving a charge of US$2,100 and a reduced value of US$4,900, and so on. See Straight line depreciation.

Registered auditors Auditors who are registered by the organisation which controls auditing activities. This body can be the government (Ministry of Finance) or the professional regulatory body.

Repatriation of profits The sending back to a foreign parent company of profits earned by a subsidiary company. This is normally done by paying dividends but can also take the form of repayment of capital (where capital is legally reduced).

Reporting Has several meanings: a verbal or written account of an event; a subordinate is said to report to his superior or *boss*, i.e. he is responsible to or *reports to* his *boss*. *Reporting lines* is a term used in organisation charts to show lines of responsibility from lower to higher levels of management.

Reported cost A cost which has been entered in the accounting system and is now reported, verbally or in writing

Research and development Expenditure on research for new products and on the development of prototypes through to the launching of new products

Retained profits The balance of profit remaining after payment of dividends and transfers to reserves, and which is reinvested in the business

Return on capital Profit as a percentage of the average capital employed. It is the principal measure of the profitability of a company. Note that there are various ways of defining both profit and capital employed for this calculation.

Returned goods Goods supplied to a customer and then physically returned to the supplier

Sales The value of goods and services invoiced to customers less any sales discounts

Sales and profit forecasts Revisions of the expected profit or loss for the year made by a company at regular intervals

Sales and Purchases Ledgers The records of financial transactions with customers (Sales Ledger) and suppliers (Purchase Ledger)

Sales discounting The offering of discounts or price reductions in order to increase sales

Sales tax A tax levied on the invoiced value of a sale

Security A condition of safety or reliability against business threat or loss. The physical protection of a company's assets, personnel and operations. Protection for lenders against default by a borrower (see also 'collateral')

Self-financing An activity which obtains its finance from the cash flow arising from its own operation

Selling expenses Expenses with materials, labour and overhead arising in a company's selling operations

Share The unit of value which denotes a shareholder's investment in a limited liability company

Share capital The amount of money directly invested by shareholders of a limited liability company, usually in the form of cash (can also be in the form of assets or know-how). The amount on which payment of dividends is calculated

Shareholders People or organisations which invest in a company, who are called the 'Members' and who are the owners of the company

Shareholders' equity Also known as the shareholders' *interest*. See 'equity'.

Shareholders' Meeting A meeting of shareholders held in accordance with the statutes (regulations) of the company or the laws of a country

Short-term loans Loans which are repayable within 12 months. Also includes that portion of a long-term loan which is repayable within the next 12 months

Software for accounting Computer software for processing all financial transactions through to the production of financial statements and analyses

Sourcing The procurement or obtaining of goods and services

Statement of Accounting Policies UK Company law requires limited liability companies to include in the Annual Accounts a full statement of their accounting policies on specified topics, e.g depreciation, stock valuation, foreign exchange transactions.

Statistical research The gathering of data for purposes of statistical examination as a part of a wider research project

Statutory accounts The financial statements, which UK company law requires limited companies to submit at the end of their financial year. These accounts must also contain several reports, e.g. the Audit report.

Statutory financial reports This is a broader term which covers the submission of statutory accounts but may also refer to reports required by other UK laws or regulations e.g. the Directors' Report.

Sterling The pound sterling is the formal name for the UK currency

Stock Exchange The place where investors, their brokers and dealers meet to transact the purchase and sale of stocks, shares and securities

Stock Stores of materials or goods held for resale

Stock – Inventories The listing of such stores giving the values of each item

Stock – Shares in a Company Shares in limited liability companies or corporations. In the USA the term 'common stock' is used.

Stock – Farm Animals Livestock which are created and sold for profit

Straight line depreciation A fixed asset may be assumed to lose value by the same amount each year. If a machine has a life of 5 years, then each year it would be depreciated by $1/5$ of the original cost.

Subsidiary A company controlled by another company which either owns a majority of the shares or exercises full management control

Sub-contractor A person or company which performs part of the work of another company relating to the manufacture of a product or service

Supplier A person or business which supplies goods or services to a company is referred to in accounting terms as a supplier or as a trade creditor.

Tangible fixed assets Long-term assets which have a physical presence, e.g. land, buildings, machines, vehicles. But note that investments in other companies are also sometimes described as tangible fixed assets.

Target return on capital The percentage return on capital which the management or investor expects or forecasts

Targeting of key markets The focusing or management and material resources upon specific markets considered to be of great ('key') importance to a company.

Tax – Corporation tax The tax on the profits of a business. In the UK this term refers to tax on the profits of limited companies ('corporations')

Tax – Profit or Profits tax As for Corporation tax. This term is no longer used in the UK, but is used in other countries to describe the taxation of business profits.

Tax – Withholding tax A tax which is deducted or withheld by the payer of a royalty, dividend or interest charge. The tax is paid directly to the tax authority.

Tax – Sales tax A tax calculated on the monetary or invoice value of a sale

Tax – Value added tax A system of taxation of the profit or value added arising from a company's trading activities. The suppliers collect the tax from their customers and pay it to the government. But they can first offset against it any similar taxes which they have paid to their own suppliers. Thus in effect, the tax falls only on the margin or *value added.*

Tax – Tax penalty A penalty which the tax authority imposes on a taxpayer or a company for an infringement of a tax regulation

Tax on dividends being sent out of the country When payments of dividend, interest, royalty etc. are remitted outside the country, tax is withheld by the payers and paid to their tax authority.

Taxation, double taxation of subsidiaries A foreign subsidiary company will pay tax on its profits to its own government. These profits will also suffer tax in the country of the parent company, unless the two countries have made a treaty to avoid double taxation.

Taxation and dividend regulations Laws and regulations which dictate what tax will be payable when a dividend is declared and paid. In many countries dividends are paid 'net of tax', i.e. tax is deducted by the company which is paying the dividend and paid over to the tax authority. authority. The shareholder receives a net amount.

Taxation treaty An agreement between sovereign countries governing taxation matters arising from their commercial relationship

Taxes payable See Current Liabilities – Taxes Payable

Third party Another person or company besides the two principals to an agreement

Trade discounts A percentage reduction of the prices paid

Trading licence A permission to carry on a business activity which can be given to an individual, a company or a government body

Translation of assets The conversion into the currency of the country of a parent company of all assets denominated in a foreign currency, whether shown in the books of the parent company or one of its subsidiaries

Treasury Department A department which is responsible for the provision and use of finance for a company. It includes the provision of capital, long and short-term borrowing, foreign currency management, banking, cash collection and the investment of surplus funds in money markets

Treasury Management The management of a company's financing activities carried out by a Treasury department

Treasury Management, foreign exchange risk The control or minimisation of the risk of loss from foreign currency transactions

Trial balance A list of the balances of all the accounts in the General or Nominal Ledger which proves that the accounting system is in balance, i.e. the total of all the debit balances equals the total of all the credit balances.

Turnover The total value of a company's sales. Also denotes the rate of use of an asset, e.g. stock turnover rate (dividing annual sales by the value of stock tells you how many times

	the stock was 'turned over' in the year)
Turnover tax	A tax calculated on the value of net sales (gross sales less sales discounts), e.g. sales tax (USA). Similar to a value added tax, which is calculated in the same way.
UK statutory accounts	The accounting reports which are required each year by the UK Companies Acts
Unit costs	The cost of a unit, e.g. a product, a service, an inspection, an hour of direct labour, a litre of petrol
Unquantified claim	A legal claim against a company for damages or loss, which has not yet been expressed in monetary or other terms. Such a claim may be reported as a contingent liability, which would only be shown as an actual liability when the claim has succeeded in law and can be valued.
Value added	Any material or service which is added to a basic product or service in order to increase sales income and hence profits
Value added services	A service which is added to a product or other service e.g. a technical maintenance or technical support service
Value added tax	See Tax – Value added tax
Variable cost	A cost which tends to vary with the level of sales or business activity e.g. cost of materials
Wages/ salaries	Payments made to permanent employees, whether full-time or part-time. UK companies pay *wages* weekly to manual workers, and *salaries* monthly for clerical and management staff.
Withdrawing of capital	The reduction of share capital of a company, e.g the repatriation of share capital by a foreign subsidiary
Withholding tax	A tax which is deducted from a gross amount e.g. a dividend or a royalty payment, and paid to the tax authority
Work in progress	Unfinished manufactured products or services
Working capital	The capital available for the daily operations of a company. Normally the investment in working capital is measured by the excess of current assets over current liabilities.
Write off	To bring the value of an asset to zero, either by removing it from the account in which it stands or by establishing a provision equivalent to its book value
Write down	To reduce the value of an asset to its estimated market or realisable value, by setting up a provision which will reduce the original value to the level required.
Write back	To reverse a write down or write off. Example : if a doubtful debt for which a provision has been created against non-payment is subsequently paid, then the provision is no longer required and can be credited back to the Profit and Loss Account.

Index

SUBJECT AND VOCABULARY

Notes:

1 A page number followed by **d** means that the word can be found in the dialogue on that page. You may have to look in the corresponding tapescript to find the word.

2 Page numbers show only where words occur. For fuller explanations, look in the Glossary.

3 It is customary to spell all index entries with initial capital letters as though they are the first words of sentences. Otherwise, when writing, small letters may be used, apart from titles of particular people such as the Financial Controller and certain financial documents such as the Balance Sheet and the Profit and Loss Account. These rules apply in addition to the usual rules for using capital letters in English.

Accounting information, purpose of providing 99**d**, 108, 109
Accounting Law 108, 109
Accounting obligations 86**d**, 99**d**, 109, 120

Accounting period 17,(financial year, 138)
Accounting policies 109, 111, 118, 120,125
Accounting procedures 109
Accounting principles 65, 71**d**, 75
Accounting ratios 45,56, See also Profit and Loss Ratios, 45,49**d**
Accounting regulations 108, 112, 120
Accounting staff 100
Accounting standards 85**d**, 86**d**, 125
  Directives of the European Community 109
  International 109
Accounts for management control 139
Accounts Manager 128
Acquisitions 76
Activities = cost drivers or overhead expenditures 65
Activity Costing 56, 65, 71**d**, 72**d**
Administration costs 17, 42
Analysts (financial journalists) 94, 95
Annual accounts 81, 88, 89, 118
  Responsibility of the directors for 120
Annual audit 140
Annual Report 88, 89
Application of the law 109, 111
Appointment of agents 134
Assembly line 42, 56
Assets 21, 76, 125
Associated company 71**d**, 125
At cost 125
Audit
  Content 100**d**
  Layout 100**d**
  Report 60, 99**d**
  Testing of a financial system 99**d**
Audited assets and liabilities 125
Auditing and Internal Control 140
Auditing practice 99**d**
Auditing requirements 99**d**, 100**d**
Auditing standards 99**d**,119,120
Auditors 120
Auditors, appointment of 99**d**
Auditor's Report 88, 89, 99**d**, 118, 119
Audits, post-implementation 76
Autumn Budget 129**d**, 130
Average net capital employed 49**d**

Balance sheet 16, 20**d**, 21, 24**d**, 56, 57, 139
Balance sheet analysis 44, 49**d**

Balance Sheet Ratios 44, 45, 49**d**
  See earnings per share and return on capital
  Receivables 51**d**
Bank balance 20, 21, 22
Basis of preparation of Accounts 125
Board meeting 8**d**
Board of Directors' report 89
Book-keeping obligations 109
Borrowing costs 24, 25
Borrowing guaranteed 81, 82, 86**d**
Break-even point 5,14, 30
Budget 62, 63
Budgeted cost 65
Business evaluations 75, 76
Business targets 31, 134

Capital, problem of borrowing 75
Capital employed (balance sheet item) 20**d**, 24d
Capital project, Group requirements for 76
Cash flow 30, 44
Cash flow statement 89
Cash position 97
Central Accounting Book 140, 142
Central Accounting System 138, 141
Central Bank 109, 111
Chairman 35, 62, 49, 51, 64, 89, 93, 109
Chancellor of the Exchequer 129**d**
Charge against revenue 126
Chartered Accountants 119

Chief accountant as auditor 140
Closing Inventory 17,19, 36
Collateral 85**d**
Commercial and technological obsolescence 125
Companies, overseas, subsidiary, associated 125
Company accounts, compliance with the law 109, 119, 120
Consolidated accounts 89, 120, 125
  Balance sheet 89,114**d**
  Profit and Loss Account 89
Contingent liabilities 81, 82, 84, 86**d**, 88, 97
Contributing activities 65
Conversion (of foreign exchange) 62, 114**d**
Convert 63
Corporation tax 131**d**
Corrected actual cost 65
Cost accounting system 65,71**d**
Cost driver 65
Cost driver rate 65
Cost of sales 17,18, 19, 36
Costing 58
  Methodological errors in 65
  Methods 65, 75
  Records 44, 71**d**, 72**d**
  Section 139
  Solutions to problems of 65
  System 56, 65, 71**d**, 72**d**
Costs of production 25**d**, 42**d**
Country risk 76, 79, 80
  Index for analysis of 80
Crash sale 85**d**
Creditors 20, 81
Cross guarantee 86**d**
Current assets 21, 22, 24**d**, 25**d**
Current inventory 45, 46
Current liabilities 21, 24**d**
Customer receivables 44, 25**d**, 51-52**d**

Day Books 139
Debtors 21
Depreciation 125,131**d**
Desk research 57, 58, 75
Desk review 140
Directives 104
Direct labour costs 144
Directors' responsibilities for accounts 120
Disclosure 81, 82, 108, 109
Discount sales 37
Distributorships 134, 135
Diversification 89
Dividends 24**d**, 89, 94,
  Remitting/repatriating 129**d**
Domestic competition 57
Double taxation treaty 62, 63, 88
Duties 130

Earnings per share 49**d**, 89, 62, 63
Emerging market economies 104
Employment policy 89, 134
Entrepreneurs 109, 111
Estimated useful lives 125
Eurodollar 86**d**
European Union 57, 58, 109, 111
EU, The 57, 58, 109, 111
Exchange losses, exposure to 114**d**
Exchange rates 113**d**, 114**d**, 125, 144**d**
Expansion strategy 104
Expenses 72**d**
Expertise 134,135
Exposure to foreign exchange risk 93, 103, 113**d**, 114**d**
External customers 125

Factory overheads 17, 18, 36
Fall in profits 15
Financial Accounting 138
Financial catchphrases used by journalists 95
Financial costs 44
Financial plan 6, 49**d**
Financial records 89, 99**d**
Financial system and controls 99**d**
Financial targets 57
Financial year 71**d**, 89, 138
Financing expansion 31
Financing local assets by local borrowing 114**d**
Financing strategy 113**d**
Finished goods 22
Fitting department 65, 68
Fixed Assets 20**d**, 21, 22, 125,126
  capital assets 76, 114
  land and buildings 21
  plant and equipment 21
  vehicles 21
Fixed capital acquisitions 76
Fixed costs 30, 104
Fixed overheads 144
Flagship product 31, 57, 88, 97
Fluctuations 85**d**
  in exchange rates 144**d**
Forecasts 89
Foreign currency assets 125
Foreign currency borrowings 62, 114**d**
Foreign exchange 62, 63, 103, 113
Foreign interest rates 93
Formal audit 140

GAAP 109, 111
Gearing 94, 111, 113**d**, 114**d**
Generally accepted principles (GAAP) 109
General ledger 71**d**
Gross margins 8, 11, 20**d**, 24**d**, 25**d**, 29
Gross profit 6, 7, 11, 13**d**, 17, 19, 36, 46
Group Board 76, 86**d**, 89, 92, 104
Group Business Planning Department 104
Group Chairman 49, 75
Group Export Manager 31
Group Financial Director 86**d**
Group guidelines for business evaluations 76
Guarantee, parent company 85**d**
Group directors 85

Group Main Board 30, 31, 86**d**, 88, 89
Group Managing Director 62
Group of companies 6, 7, 89
Group policy 44, 57
Guarantees 85**d**

Hedge against long-term exchange risk 114**d**
Historical cost convention 125
Historical data 65

Industrial costing 138
Intellectual property rights 81, 82
Interest costs 17, 19
Internal control 140
Internal management reporting 16
International accounting standard 88
Inventories 20**d**, 21, 22, 25**d**, 45
Inventory control 138, 140
Investment in product research 104

Joint venture 5, 30, 76, 88

Labour costs 17, 19, 36
Land and buildings 20**d**
Law relating to disclosure publication, auditing 109
Letter of Comfort 85**d**, 86**d**
Levels of stock items 140
Liabilities 21
Liberalisation, economic 117, 129**d**
Limited company 6, 7
Local borrowings 62, 63
Local currency 63, 114**d**,
  Assets 114
  Borrowing 85**d**, 113**d**, 114**d**, 115
Local sourcing of materials 144
Long-term asset acquisitions 76
Long-term financing strategy 113**d**
Long-term investment strategy 131

Main Board 86**d**
Maintenance 68, 135
Management accounts 6, 7, 16
Management team 56
Management training 134
Managing Director 6, 7, 8, 56, 62, 76
Manufacturing costs reduced by local sourcing 134
Manufacturing overheads 126
Margin 21
Margins 8**d**, 23, 57
Market penetration 31, 35
Market share 29, 134
Marketing Manager 56, 57, 75
Marketing targets 57
Material costs 45
Material handling and storage 25, 68
Material procurement 65, 68
Memorandum 65, 76
Memorandum, Head Office 31, 56, 57
Mergers 76

Minicomputer 138
Multinational 5

Net assets 108
Net profit 6, 7, 9**d**, 17, 30, 36, 62,
  As a percentage of sales 19
Nominal or General Ledger 140
Notes to the Accounts 81, 89, 97

Offset 62, 63, 114
Opening inventory 17, 18, 36
Operating expenses 11, 13, 17, 19, 36,
  Administration 20**d**, 36
  Interest costs 20**d**, 36
  Selling 36
Options for export strategy 30
Outward investment 97
Overdraft 25**d**
Overheads 13**d**, 21, 144
Overheads, allocation of 65
Overseas expansion strategy 103, 104

Packing 68
Parent company 85**d**, 86**d**, 115
Parent company guarantee 85**d**
Participants on the market 109, 111
Payables 21, 22
Payroll 138
Payroll Department 141
Penalty tax 129**d**, 130
P/E ratio 94
Personal Accounts 139
Plant and equipment 20**d**
Post implementation audits 76
Presentation of Accounting Information 99**d**, 109, 139
Principle of Going Concern 109, 111
Procurement 57, 58
Product factor (as a cost driver) 65
Product liability 81, 82
Product range 94, 97
Production costing 8**d**, 11, 13**d**, 20**d**, 65
Production Manager 56, 57, 75
Production runs 42, 44
Production setting-up 42, 65, 68
Production targets 140
Profit 5, 8d, 13**d**, 21, 24, 25**d**, 30, 38, 75, 89, 104, 134
  net 5, 6, 8d, 43,
  gross 6, 11, 13d, 16, 18, 20**d**, 44
Profit and Loss Statement/Account 5, 12, 13**d**, 16, 18, 19, 36
Profit after tax 134
Profit before tax (pre-tax profit) 16, 17, 18, 36
Profit contribution 37
Profit forecast 62
Profit and Loss Account 13**d**, 15, 17, 56, 57
Profit and Loss ratios
  Factory Overheads 44, 45
  Gross Profit 44, 45
  Material costs 44, 45
  Selling and administrative expenses 44, 45, 49**d**
Prospects 62, 63

Public limited company 6, 8**d**
Purchases 17, 19, 36

Quantity discounts 42**d**
Quality control 65, 68
Quarterly Management Meeting 62

Raising capital 75, 85**d**, 86, 88
Rationalisation 89, 104
Rationalising 89
Raw materials 21, 22, 25**d**, 45, 46
Receivables 20, 21, 46
Recession 6, 7, 8**d**
Registered Auditors 119
Repatriation of profits 129**d**, 130, 131**d**, 144**d**
Reported costs 65
Reported global earnings 93
Reporting on product profitability 11, 13**d**
Research and Development 126
Retained profits 21
Return on capital 8**d**, 11, 18, 24**d**, 49**d**, 131**d**

Sales 17, 19
Sales and Profit Forecast 37
Sales and Purchase ledgers 140
Sales discounting 45, 46
Sales tax 125, 129**d**, 130
Security 85**d**
Self-financing 94
Selling and administrative expenses 45
Selling costs 19
Share 93, 94
Share capital 20, 89
Shareholders 24**d**, 89, 119
Shareholders' equity 21, 22
Shareholders' meeting 15, 89
Short-term loans 21
Software for accounting 138
Sourcing 134, 135
Statement of Accounting Policies 89
Statutory accounts 85**d**, 99**d**, 100**d**
Statutory financial reports 140
Statutory requirements 100**d**
Sterling 86**d**, 114**d**, 125
Stock Exchange, the 6, 7**d**
Stocks 126
Straight line depreciation 131**d**
Subsidiary 5, 6, 22, 30, 71**d**, 86**d**, 104
Sub-contractor 8
Supplier 6, 7
    local sourcing of materials 134, 144**d**

Tangible fixed assets 125
Target return on capital 57
Targeting of key markets 104
Task force 43**d**, 44, 57, 75
Tax, allowances 131**d**
    Corporation 129**d**, 130
    Sales 129**d**, 130
    Withholding 129**d**, 130
    Value added 129**d**, 130
    Penalty 129**d**, 130
Tax payable on profits 21
Taxation, double taxation of subsidiaries 88
Taxation and dividend regulations 118
Taxation treaty 88
Taxes 140
Taxes payable 20
Terms of reference 57, 58
Third parties 76
Total cost of sales 36
Trade creditors 25**d**
Trade discounts 21, 125
Trading licence 100
Translation of assets 125
Treasury Department 85
Treasury Management 113**d**
    and foreign exchange risk 103
Trial balances 140
Turnover 5, 6, 7, 25**d**, 30, 125

UK statutory accounts 85
Unit costs 42**d**, 44, 65, 139,
    Presentation of information about
Units of production 144
Unquantified claims 81, 82

Value added services in the areas of maintenance,
    training and development 134
Value Added Tax 125, 130
Vehicles 21

Wages 140
Withdrawal of capital 131**d**
Withholding of tax 131**d**
Work in progress 22
Working capital 11, 62, 63
Write-off 125

LANGUAGE

Adjective-noun phrases 22
Admonishing or prescribing 47
Adverbial phrases 29
Advising and recommending 69
Allowing thinking time 52
As and *while* 143
As shown by 84
Asking the bank for credit 103, 114**d**

Before + verb + *ing* 70
By means of 137
By .... to 18

Calculations
    Language for 19
    Talking about 23
Cohesion through use of equivalent expressions 83
Collocations 26

Commenting 40
Concession shown by using 'while' 98
Connectors 39, 54, 64, 69, 111, 112, 116
  Cohesion 83, 84
  Purposive *to* 137
  Through 107
  While/as 143
Continuous past actions leading to the present situation 28

Decide that and *decide to* 34, 35
Defining participles 41, 123
Defining relative clauses 123
Definite article 48, 59
Delaying what you are going to say 52
Denying possibility 41
Despite 9
Determiners 48
  the articles 59

Either/or 143
Equivalence 50
Explaining and comparing 99
Expressing compulsion 101
Expressing purpose 40

Financial catchphrases used by journalists 95
Financial noun phrases 77
First conditional 116
Forecasts 89
Formal language 68, 110, 111
Future simple 116

Grammatical cohesion devices 84
  Have to 101

If (first conditional) 116
Immediate action, suggesting 52
Impersonal decision-making 33
Impersonal passive 34
Impersonal sentences 59
In preparing/to prepare 111
Incomplete sentences in a statement of aims 137
Indefinite article 48, 59
Indirect speech and thought 40
  About current events 26, 40, 98
  About definite future events 27
  About doubtful events 26
  About prior events 27
Indirect statements 26, 27
Indirect thoughts, feelings and perceptions 26-8
Informal language 68, 110 111
Instrumental by 70
Intention 137
Intransitive verbs 10,11
It has/there is 20, 142

Language for calculation 19
Let's + verb 52
Logical connectors 64
Memoranda 31, 56, 57

Modals followed by *unless* 99

Need to 83
Noun phrases 33, 100
Numbers, practice with 18

Obligation 106

Passives 34, 92, 122, 123, 141, 142
Past actions leading to present results 26, 28
Percentages 19
Periods of time, expressing 40
Persuade 83, 117
Possibility 87
Prepositions 35, 63, 78, 107, 128
Present continuous with already 97
Present perfect 28, 69, 107, 120
Present perfect continuous 27
Present perfect passive 107
Present simple 117
  for stating rules or acts 112
  for giving explanations 92
Purpose, expressing 40
Purposive *to* 69, 111, 116, 137

Relative pronoun, ommiting 8
Reported actions 124
Reported directives and recommendations 59

Sentence connectors 39
  reason, result, contrast, time sequence 69
Shall and *will* 112, 137
Should 33
Simple past conditions 53
Simple present conditions 53
Simultaneous actions 70
Softening negative comment 142
Style 46
Suggesting immediate action 52
Suggesting possibility 87
Synonyms 67

There is/are, was/were, has/have been 19, 142
Through 116, 137
Through used to mean *by means of* 107, 137
To prepare/in preparing 111
Transitive verbs 10, 11

Understanding and agreement 26
Unless present + future 98, 99

Which 69, 107, 123
  omission of 8, 107, 123
While 98
While and *as* 143
Will and *shall* 112, 137
Word families 66

Zero determiner 59